# Take Action

## A Self-Made Millionaire's Pocket Guide
to Business Success

# The Author

Stephen Joynes is the President of Barons Holdings Spas and Resorts Ltd, including Hoar Cross Hall, a one-time run down stately home which he bought in 1989 and turned into a multi-million pound industry-leading Spa Resort and Eden Hall, Newark, bought in 1998. He is a nationally renowned self-made businessman; has been the subject of a Central TV documentary The Millionaires and provided a lead feature for Hello magazine. He is married with one son, and lives on the Hoar Cross Hall estate near Lichfield, Staffordshire.

First published in Great Britain 1997
Reprinted 2002
Reprinted 2003
Reprinted 2004

© Copyright Stephen Joynes 1997

All rights reserved.

No part of this publication may be reproduced, stored in any retrieval system, or transmitted, in any form or by any means without prior permission in writing from the publisher, nor be otherwise circulated in any form of binding or cover other that in which it is published and without a similar condition including this condition being imposed on the subsequent purchaser, except in accordance with the provisions of the Copyright, Designs and Patents Act 1988.

ISBN 0 9531354 0 3


Printed and bound in Great Britain
by Freedman Brothers Printers Limited
26 St Albans Lane
London NW11 7QE
020 8458 3220

Hello to my readers and friends,
especially to those who, despite all setbacks,
achieve success through taking action,
making something special happen in their lives.

To my team of happy, enthusiastic professionals,
and all of my family and friends who have
joined in with my actions along the way
most of whom have progressed happily
along with me.

I wish you all continued success

# How did an eleven-plus failure manage to write a book like this?

I wrote my first, and what I thought would be my only book, at the age of 22. *Selling Yourself* was not a great commercial success or what you could ever call a 'classic'. It did however, detail what I, as a young man, believed were the essential principles and actions required to be successful. I followed my advice and achieved, by my own expectations, unbelievable success.

Many years and a number of successful enterprises later, I was being approached by magazines, the Marketing Institute and on more than one occasion by TV stations, to review my life and provide personal views and experiences.

To prepare, I wrote many notes of what were my obvious moves and actions. I detailed the main steps and the enjoyment I had experienced en-route. After interviews, I was often asked the same question, "Why don't you write a book?" I had my notes and my original book, so it seemed that I was halfway there. It wasn't quite that easy, but nothing worthwhile ever is.

I'm humbled to think that my views are considered worthy

of print and whenever this book helps anyone to greater success it will give me great satisfaction.

I must point out this is not a business text book, there are far more qualified theorists than I to write those. It is a collection of my thoughts, actions and observations on what has led me to where I am today.

Please enjoy reading this book, absorb the principles and above all else, *Take Action*. Then you can be a great success and enjoy the fruits of your labour.

# Contents

# Section One
# Your Finest Asset

# What a wonderful world

*Plan now to enjoy your future and take advantage of all available opportunities.*

Today, many people have far more spending power than they had 40 or 50 years ago, then being poor meant you had no shoes or went without food. Today, we take so much for granted – then, cars, televisions or even a choice of clothes and shoes were only for the rich.

Having this additional disposable income means that people spend more money on the pleasures of life, whether it's adventure holidays, wind-down Spa breaks or hobbies. This opens up the market to include opportunities for you. Business opportunities now flourish that would have otherwise failed miserably, due to a lack of support from a population that couldn't afford them.

Today the world really is your oyster, take action and make your ideas grow successfully.

This book will give you choices and options. It will be up to you to decide how much you want to change your future. Success means something different to everyone - the choice is yours.

Change your future by your own efforts and even if you end up with only double what you have now, it will have been well worth the effort.

If you want more, then you have to push yourself harder, using your hidden talents and abilities to transform your life.

**Take action now and start to make your ideas grow into unbelievable future success.**

# Born with a silver spoon – hardly!

**A** two-up two-down rented terrace house in Walsall with water and toilet across the yard, gas lamps, no electricity. I had oversized wellies and at one stage a pair of football boots with the studs removed and cobbled on heels, my dad grew vegetables and kept pigeons, chickens and rabbits which supplemented our diet – "we certainly were not poor! – or hungry!" My Dad generally arrived home around 6pm. Mum would say "Your dinner's ready!" He would say "I'll just check my pigeons." His dinner went on a plate on top of the saucepan, around two hours later he would return from his beloved pigeons.

He must have caught my development bug before I did, because he continually extended his pigeon lofts, sometimes to the dismay of the neighbours.

The richest man in our street had an old motor car he polished on Sundays but hardly ever drove – ah the good old days.

I caught diphtheria at five and scarlet fever at seven, spending over a month in an isolation hospital (as a little lost soul) each time with no contact with my parents or the outside world. Further illnesses including bronchitis, whooping cough, tonsillitis, yellow jaundice and other general problems kept me at home in bed. I missed a great deal of school between the most formative ages of five and twelve. All in all I had a pretty sickly and far from successful childhood. The highlights of my life at 8 and 9 were when I spent 3 weeks on a farm which catered for around 10 under privileged children whose families could not afford holidays.

I fully appreciated the exciting opportunity of working hard and enjoying it, including going into the fields by myself at dawn to pick mushrooms. These, the lovely farmer's wife cooked for our breakfasts. Sitting on the tractor by the farmer was magic!

Hay-making gave me the opportunity to swing a pitch fork

*Young Stevie Joynes in his first stately home*

and exercise at the same time – even the smell of pigsties was a taste of heaven for me. I was in paradise paddling in the pond with the cows.

Unfortunately my lack of standardised schooling meant I failed my eleven plus – I had difficulty understanding the questions let alone the answers. Fortunately my reading and spelling skills were good because I was forever reading library books whilst bedridden.

Prior to leaving school, a careers' officer asked me what sort of job I would like? "I'd like to be an archeologist", I replied. "You need a sponsor" he said. I thought this a great idea and promptly asked my dad where I could find one. "A sponsor is someone with money, and we don't know any of those" was his reply. My one exciting idea of a future job was lost and with no qualifications and few alternatives I started work with my father as a plasterers' improver.

I moved from job to job at a fairly rapid pace trying to find my niche in life. From plastering to cabinet making. At 15 I worked on the railways as an engine cleaner, not old enough to be a fireman, an extremely well paid job, I volunteered to be a 'Bar Boy' cleaning clinkers from inside the fire box of steam engines. This was an extremely hot, uncomfortable, dirty and unpopular job, but it paid twice the rate of a cleaner. The extra money allowed me to buy all of my own clothes and holidays and still have some left over. I might have been dirty but I was having fun and proud to be progressing towards a new world.

At 16 I moved back into the building trade as a general assistant, in a small firm. Most of my time was spent on carpentry but I was enthusiastic and willing to assist and help out in all areas. I also offered to do material collections on my motorbike – I was cheaper and faster than a van and driver.

As part of a team I absorbed, often subconsciously, the basic building techniques which were to become the main foundation of my future success. I enjoyed the work, it was varied and interesting, but not yet my real aim for the future.

Salvation came with National Service. Called up at the age

*Starting a new life*

of eighteen, I decided the life of a "Brylcreem Boy" in the R.A.F. would be exciting, glamourous and give me the chance to mix with people from different backgrounds. I hoped it would give me the opportunity to start changing my future life forever, luckily for me, the selection was based on an intelligence test and not an education test. I passed and became a radar operator and fighter plotter.

I concentrated upon the intensive maths crammer lessons and they taught me more in a month than I had learnt at school, I could now do percentages and fractions in a flash. Based in Germany, the R.A.F. was great fun but once again not my idea of a permanent life-style for the future. It was now obvious to me that to progress in life I had to improve my education. So I spent my free time, when not enjoying myself at the local HOF (hotel bar) or dance hall, studying a variety of correspondence courses, including; the art of conversation, psychology and best of all "The National School of Salesmanship". "I knew no salesmen – could I become one?"

Demob at twenty one brought me back to civvy street with the definite intention of being successful, but with no actual idea exactly how, or what at. So it was back to building, whilst at the same time attending interviews for sales positions. "Another life changing opportunity".

# CV of Stephen Joynes – Aged 21 years

**Biggest Liabilities**
- No experience
- No qualifications
- No money

**Biggest Assets**
- Enthusiasm
- Determination
- The will to Succeed
- A Big Smile

My passion for owning my own business and being a somebody was still growing. I advertised 'made to measure sink and kitchen units' – one way of using a skill I already had – strapping cabinets onto my back before delivering them on my motorbike I also started a by-post friendship and marriage bureau – a new type of enterprise long before its time – and called it "Friendships Unlimited". To make it sound more commercial, I put **Dept. B** before my council house address.

*Looking for any opportunity*

Advertising in shop windows was well received, unfortunately with mainly male applicants, a satisfactory conclusion was difficult to achieve. At that time, no newspapers or magazines would accept these possibly dubious adverts!! (I was just a few years too early.)

I constantly searched the business opportunities column in the local newspaper. "Mobile Fish & Chip Van for Sale, £120 o.n.o." – a business within my price range. I borrowed £50 from my mother (saying I would emigrate to Australia if she didn't lend it to me), added it to my savings and bought my chip van, refurbished and painted it. This was certainly the most major event in my life to date! I possessed only a motorcycle licence; four weeks and eight one hour lessons later I passed my driving test.

Then I was driving this huge van down a dual carriageway - WOW! When reversing, I got out every two feet - checked - still OK? etc, etc. - what an event!

I put £3 of petrol into my new mobile business, the normal week's usage for my motorbike. The next day (and only ten miles later!) it stopped. I couldn't believe it! I had run out of petrol, with my chips sizzling en route to my next location two miles away! I legged it to the nearest garage, borrowed a can, ran back and she started. Two days later it wouldn't start - a faulty battery! Could running a business really be this expensive? I could just about afford to buy the potatoes - a new battery was way out of my price range. The nice man at the garage suggested **HIRE PURCHASE** - my first financial shock.

I took H.P. - my only option - I was on yet another unexpected fast learning curve.

Steve's Chippery soon took off however, a fast way to learn all aspects of a hands-on business, finance, marketing and all other areas of being your own boss on a shoestring. I promoted it by advertising with door-to-door leaflets– "Look for the Big Cream Van with that irresistible aroma calling at _Venue_ and _Time_". I was taking control of my own destiny, my working capital was what I took on the night!

I later sold my fish and chip van for more than twice the purchase price and development cost. I sold it with so much enthusiasm ( I nearly bought it back!). This was the first time in my life that I was to be the recipient of a largish sum of money! What if the cheque bounced? That would be an unbelievable calamity. I settled for a cash cheque, took it straight to their bank and came away with a bag of money. My most exciting event to date, it was fantastic!

I put pen to paper, outlining my ideas for future success. I self-published _Selling Yourself_ and advertised it in the local paper as the simple way to teach yourself 'how to obtain a sales position'. It sold only a few dozen copies, due to an extremely limited advertising budget. Not yet a breakthrough to financial success, but at least I was making things happen, teaching myself and gathering further valuable experience for my future.

During this time, I obtained my my first sales position selling office equipment and then moved rapidly through a number of often commission only daytime sales jobs. My policy was only to borrow money that I could invest into an appreciating asset. With minimum outlay I purchased a beyond-its-best GPO van with ladder rack for £20. Painting it a pale blue, this made a reasonable impact on my current credit drapery round, which was then followed by trading stamps, and advertising space. I then progressed to a more upmarket position with Eskimo Frozen Foods. I now had a weekly salary, an Eskimo van and a regular round of shopkeepers who sometimes even wanted to buy before I sold them something – "A different world". I progressed through the company with pride. I was good at opening new accounts, so they sent me around the country on sales drives.

The Posh hotels I stayed in perhaps helped me to subconsciously understand and have a liking for the Hotel trade. I was promoted to manager, leading and motivating a team of reps in the Birmingham area. My benefits included a nice car, commission, job satisfaction and a future.

I eventually decided I had found my niche in life at the age of 26. I had bought a tea shop and redeveloped it into a café selling grills all day (novel in the days before McDonalds). I kept my day job at Eskimo and company car, selling my house to buy the café after persuading a bank manager to lend me £1,000 – my first business loan! They wanted £200 more for the café than I could raise. They were going to buy a house. I had a house, I offered it to them at an asking price of £2,200 then reduced the price by £200, if they would do the same. They wanted to sell and I wanted to buy so we agreed prices and did a swap. I was on the business property ladder.

Using my hands-on building skills I created "The Golden Grill", proved its potential, then sold it around twelve months later for more than twice what it cost me.

This could be my route to future success, buy a rundown, hands-on, people-to-people business or property. Redesign, build and develop it, prove its profit potential then sell it for more than twice what it cost!

Next came a semi-derelict guest house that I turned into the 15-bedroom Midland Hotel and again sold eighteen months later for more than twice its cost. I lived in one room during the development stage, without the luxury of a bathroom. Each evening I knocked holes in walls to update it and make it more like a small luxury Hotel. Situated in a rundown area at the back of the station it eventually became an Oasis in a Wilderness. Marks & Spencers were opening a new store and required accommodation for their key opening staff. "I was their man", as they reduced in number, my other guests increased.

I was interviewed by Eskimo Food's personnel manager who wanted me to apply for a Regional Manager's position. This would have entailed me moving house. I was still creating the Midland Hotel, therefore this would have been most inconvenient. I decided it was probably the right time to move on.

I applied for a management position with Green Shield Trading Stamps. They said they liked me, but their policy was to always promote through the ranks. Would I be willing to start as a Salesman? providing I hit all the targets they set me for the first four months, they would promote me to Area Manager. I took the gamble and started again at the bottom. Selling not just stamps, but also "Stamp Usage". I achieved my targets and became an Area Manager.

When Green Shield discovered I was the owner of the Midland Hotel they decided to test my loyalty, they transferred me from the West Midlands to be Manager of the East Midlands. I enjoyed the travelling and staying in top hotels. But it was interfering with my future property dreams. I left and became a vending machine salesman with Autobars.

Prior to selling the Midland, I took advantage of another opportunity. With enthusiasm and optimism, I'd bought an empty private school and began converting it into the three star County Hotel – while now working as a commission-only salesman for Autobars Vending, thankfully earning enough to pay the bricklayers' weekly wages.

I experienced an unbelievable feeling of excitement and fear when I drove past and saw the mixer turning, knowing that I must pay all of the costs from my commission-only earnings.

Working on the County Hotel development most afternoons, but especially each weekend, as a hands-on foreman with a large assortment of part-time tradesmen. Before its completion, I won the award 'Autobars' salesman of the year'. The Midland I could cope with in my spare time, but opening this larger hotel meant going full-time into the hotel business, with no time for a back-up job. It was now **make it or bust**.

I became a total hands-on hotel developer, day-to-day manager, Head Barman, Cashier, Receptionist and leader of a team in a business that I had no real experience of.

I quickly learnt the ups and downs of the Hospitality Trade. Eventually creating three further major hotel developments and selling each on for bigger and bigger profits. Leading by example, nothing was ever too much trouble if it made my guests happy – I made a policy decision then to always make "Any Reasonable Request a Pleasure" with my pen and paper always on hand to help me to remember.

Four years and four extensions later the County Hotel was exceedingly successful. I even sometimes had time to put my feet up on my desk. An opportunity for another trial chapter in my life.

This materialised into a 3 year partnership with another developer, giving both of us an insight into a more corporate business style i.e. joint shareholding and joint decisions. Together we created the Château Impney Hotel and Conference Centre

Another fast learning curve of working on a larger scale, with interior designers and consultants, Holding Companies, Group Trading, Financial Advisers and Corporate Finance – a "different world". But also a more expensive one!

I enjoyed most of the challenge but was extremely happy with the sell-out which coincided with my birthday and a champagne dinner in a hotel which was no longer my problem!

I was delighted to be on my own again, nice suits, nice car, nice house, but no office or staff. I was restarting from scratch.

Aged 37, I was a man of independent means looking for another challenging opprtunity in life, at the peak of an economic boom cycle. With property hard to find, I bought a semi-derelict nightclub, this became Barons Court Hotel, 14 years and 14 extensions later. When, mainly because I was told by the planners that due to already building on most of my land, I would not be able to create any more extensions. I started looking for an alternative site.

I contacted many agents, one of whom informed me that he also had an empty Stately Home for sale! A Stately Home! When I toured its 70 rooms, I experienced an unbelievable inner excitement! Could it be possible, a boy from a poor background owning a Stately Home? I could make it come true, but could I take the risk of achieving an unusual one-off enterprise way out in the countryside?

I bit the bullet and decided to go for it. After agreeing the purchase, I decided the many exceptional offers I was receiving for Baron's Court were too good to miss, especially because the two initial development years at Hoar Cross would allow me no spare time to continue overseeing the day-to-day operations at Barons Court.

The other Health Farm operators laughed when they heard that I was going to create a cocktail bar, that my guests would dress elegantly for dinner, to enjoy extensive à la carte dining. I created a **Paradise Spa** that my wife and I would have enjoyed staying at. My guests loved it and we became the only Health Spa Resort in a Stately Home in Britain! An ongoing exciting adventure.

## Where I am Now

I have progressed on to what I have always really wanted. I

now concentrate mainly on developing my property company Spa and Resort Developments Ltd. Plus of course controlling: FUTURE PLANNING PROJECTIONS, DESIGNING AND OVERSEEING EXTENSIONS, ALL POLICY AND PRICING DECISIONS, MAINTAINING STANDARDS, STAFF MOTIVATION AND RESOLVING EVERY UNUSUAL OCCURRENCE ETC ETC, leaving the normal day-to-day operations of Hoar Cross Hall in the capable hands of my experienced management team, most of whom have been with me for many years, having been promoted through the ranks. This is my standard practice, giving my friendly, willing staff incentive bonuses and excellent opportunities for advancement.

The opening of our son Steve's dream venture – Eden Hall Day Spa, sees the culmination for him of nearly 5 years of extremely hard work, it really had its roots in his young childhood....

At the age of eight he drew plans, along with cars and strange shaped houses with coiled wire for smoke out of its chimney, of vast hotels and leisure complexes with elaborate features, paying particular attention to detail.

As he matured he still had so much enthusiasm for creating something, but he was frustrated because he did not know what! All the unusual ideas Steve put to me proved not quite viable, although I did always encourage him to keep on thinking, whilst continuing to work hard.

After three years of working together in my office, he was convinced of the benefits, for both of us, if we were to have our own offices. I realised from this point on that it was the start of a new beginning for him.

This reminded me of the time when Steve was about eight, asking if I minded being called 'Dad' not 'Daddy', and the same lump appeared in my throat.

The conception of Eden Hall Day Spa entailed a year to find the suitable property, two further years taken to obtain planning permission and nearly two years of in depth design and development. He also has top management who trained and gained their hands on experience at Hoar Cross Hall.

The creation of relaxation was his dream, he "Took Action" and made it come true, using all the training and knowledge he had gained since leaving grammar school at 16. He had hands-on building experience at the sharp end, having worked on the Baron's Court extensions, plus personal working involvement in every hotel department including leisure, direct to the public sales experience with fitted kitchen equipment, time spent in a recruitment agency, plus further experience of every aspect of running a Health Spa and moving on to the exciting challenge of controlling the marketing of the Premier Health Spa Resort in a Stately Home.

With a natural background to the design and operation of the biggest Day Spa in the country, he now tests his knowledge and hands on ability with his own team of happy professionals.

Steve has a full and exciting way of life, making his dreams come true and enjoying the appreciation of his guests. This is a giant progress step towards a satisfying future.

Steve Junior has learnt by and survived many character building experiences. The ultimate being on the pre-opening night of Eden Hall. Everyone worked day and night for three weeks including weekends to meet the deadline promised opening date of Saturday 26th January.

On Friday at 11pm the technician doing the final check of the sophisticated fire alarm system, found a panel fault he could not rectify. A new part could not be located before Tuesday. His dream had nearly turned into a nightmare.

What could he do? He had no choice but to get his team in at 6am to start contacting guests arriving that day to re-schedule their arrivals. He also had to meet and explain the news to the arrivals his staff were unable to contact. Special gift treats were of course given to soften the blow.

What an experience for all concerned! Nevertheless a re-scheduled opening date complete with happy guests restored Steve's faith and the event was superb and welcoming.

Ordinary problems in future would never seem that bad!

He now fully enjoys his Eden Hall Day Spa, another escape

from life's pressures, bursting with quiet excitement and luxury.

My lovely wife Janet who I met almost like "Cinderella at the Ball" during a dinner dance at my Barons Court Hotel, finds time (when not looking after me!), to own and operate the "New Me Boutique" at Hoar Cross Hall. She enjoys buying for the Oasis of Happiness created by her team in her own special domain.

We now go on many relaxing happy holidays together, usually to the same hotels that we like to return to. I love my holidays but I am always happy to return.

The Spa Resort in a Stately Home, is still my favourite hobby. I continue to work hard, adding more amenities and especially enjoying the team time spent co-operating with and progressing our son's joint ventures. I also ensure that I take time out to enjoy the pleasures of my swimming pools, water grottos, aromatherapy room, saunas, saunarium, steamrooms, gymnasium, treatment rooms, golf academy, tennis courts et al. It was hard work getting here but I now take some time to fully enjoy the fruits of my labour.

**Work hard but enjoy it.**

**Don't let the grass grow under your feet.**

**Be prepared to expect the unexpected.**

# Your Finest Asset

t Hoar Cross Hall (HCH) we have a secret weapon, it costs nothing and is warmly appreciated by all of our guests, I'll let you in this simple secret, it's called a smile.

The staff at HCH are, of course, selected for their ability to do the job, but equally, if not more importantly, on their personality. It sounds glib I know, but I only employ 'nice' people. People make a business. Pleasant, friendly, happy and of course competent employees make a customer-friendly and ultimately successful business.

Business is first and foremost about people and your business is first and foremost about you and what you do – you are your finest asset. You are your main vehicle for becoming successful, and until you fully understand, believe and act on this fact, success will always be a distant dream. Most people have no problem understanding the need to improve and maintain their tangible assets; they polish and service their car, they improve or extend their property. Success in your chosen career or business is ultimately down to you constantly polishing, improving and extending your skills and ability, leading and guiding your team.

Success begins when you decide with conviction that you will be successful. Success is achieved through a sustained and committed effort to improve yourself.

## Success is down to you.

## Your options and abilities improve unbelievably as you improve yourself.

# The secrets of success – what secrets?

I'm often asked "what's the secret of your success". Well, there is no simple answer to the secret of success. It is a combination of your actions and attitude to life, unless of course you crack a code for picking the lottery numbers.

Success is the town at the end of your journey. It's up to you to decide which town you're going to. Your goal could be a big house in the country; a million in the bank; becoming the chairman of a multinational PLC. Equally, it may be having a big enough pension to retire at 60 without a drop in living standards, having first paid off your mortgage. Only you can decide what success really means to you - but achieving success requires the same steps for nearly everyone. You can transform your future by taking action starting today.

Follow the simple guidelines in this book and they will help you make more of a success of your life.

**Have a vision of your future
and then take action to make it come true.**

# Step one – decide on your destination

**M**any years ago I dreamt of having a desk with five different coloured phones. If the green phone rang, it would be my hotel in the Seychelles; the red, my hotel in the Caribbean, and so on. I did not arrive at this particular destination, but at a better one. My dream changed along the way, the idea of continually flying around the world on business no longer appealed to me. Striving towards my initial dreams has brought me to where I am now. Along the route, my ambitions changed and I altered the course I was taking.

Your dream does not have to be grand, it may be signing one particular deal, earning £50,000 next year or starting your own business. Decide now where you want to go, but be prepared to change and adjust your expectations as you progress.

Enjoy your work and it will become easier. Get satisfaction from every successful step you take.

**Decide what success really means to you.**

# Step two – Work out your route

I was now 26, and had worked out how I was going to fulfil my dreams. Buy a rundown business or property, redesign and develop it, prove its profit potential then for faster future progress sell it for more than twice the cost.

I now had a definite plan, I enjoyed creating things and was experienced in building, it was what I could be good at and enjoy at the same time. Developing hotels or property was a natural and logical route for me.

Take a careful look at your background, experiences, favourite interests and hobbies. What could you be good at and enjoy at the same time?

## What could you be good at and enjoy?

## Decide – then do it!

# Step three – Have the belief to get started and the will-power to keep going

So far so good, now for the challenging part. Making a success of anything takes time and huge amounts of effort. It's one thing having your dreams and deciding how to achieve them, most people find this fairly easy. Believing you can do it and having the conviction to keep going is where most fail.

So how can we believe and where do we get the conviction from?

With the best will in the world, if someone had told me forty years ago that I'd achieve what I have today, I would simply not have believed them. What I did believe, was what I could do tomorrow and the next day, to make progress. **Take action**, set yourself a goal – work out your first move, the next ones will gradually be more obvious and easier to decide upon.

Your great plan has to be broken down into a believable size. For example, having a dream of half a million in the bank may be difficult for you to really believe, in your current situation. If however, your plan is broken down to, this year I will make £50 profit per week after tax, next year I will use that profit to earn twice as much, the year after the same etc. In eight years this will amount to over half a million in the bank. The task becomes more believable and achievable, giving you a goal to aim at on a week-to-week basis. The difference is if the belief and conviction is fuelled by realisable achievements.

Work out what you have to do tomorrow to keep en-route for your future aims. Set yourself a goal!

**Sell yourself to yourself with conviction.**

**Have faith in yourself and your staying power.**

# Step Four – "Take action" – Making the big difference

C lichés rule in this area I'm afraid, so here's a few – Go for it!, Do it now!, Don't put off till tomorrow what you can do today!

If there is one thing above all others that will make a difference in your life, this is it – 'Take action and do Something'. Providing that something happens to be in your chosen direction, you're on your way.

Non-action, procrastination, waiting for the other person to make the first move, all add up to the same – you're going nowhere, you're treading water. Above all else, take control and make something happen – that in itself will cause something else to happen and if your chosen plan is sound you're moving forward.

In 1989 when I bought my rundown stately home with visions of developing it into the country's finest Resort Spa. The first plans were passed, the builders were busy with the redevelopment and extensions when the local authority sprang one of their many surprises. "Mr Joynes it'll take three years to upgrade the sewerage facilities at Hoar Cross to accommodate your development." Would I wait three years? Not likely, we built our own sewage works. We took action and continued to progress.

## Take control, make a decision and make things happen.

## Take small action steps now and get started.

# Summary

1. Start to think and act now, write down what success would really mean to you. Ensure you consider the important balance of the three areas of your life – business, family and personal goals.

2. Write down the outline of what sort of business you think you could be good at.

3. Write down also what you now see as the overall master plan for your future business.

4. Decide roughly what actions are needed to achieve your goals. Be prepared to fine tune them continuously, forever.

5. Break your master plan down into small achievable actions. Test the water with your first moves.

6. The toughest part is ensuring you get into the habit of taking consistent action towards achieving. Never stand still.

7. Monitor your success and progress. Change course and adapt your master plan whenever you need to.

**Make this the first chapter of your new life, then keep going.**

# The most difficult but exciting part – changing your life

As I can confirm that there's not one simple secret to success and this book would be of little value if I just reminded you of what you probably knew. The real value will come if I can convince you, through a new way of understanding, into believing that **you can change your future life** and make things different and better by **your own endeavours**.

If I could make a success with my background and education, give me, or better still yourself, one good reason why you can't. You'll be hard pushed to find a real reason, but excuses could come easy.

Convince yourself now. Your conviction must come from belief and good results obtained through your planned actions will strengthen that belief. So how do you polish and improve your number one asset to achieve these good results?

We've all been taught to believe that successful people are made, not born. That's true, but the only person who can genuinely build you into an exceptional success is **you. Yourself!**

Others can provide wise council but unless you believe you have the power to change, then no amount of information or advice will help. You simply become more expert in knowing what actions you should be taking, whilst all the time moving further and further away from taking them.

Most people are too frightened of failure and this fear is the limiting factor that stops them moving on to better things. This fear may never be admitted or in some cases acknowledged, it's normally presented as a plausible excuse or another reason to avoid taking action. If that happens to you, don't make excuses, recognise this understandable fear for what it is, it's what's stopping you from being successful. Deal with it and you're on your way, do nothing and you make your lack of progress inevitable.

**Can you change and cope with the consequences?**

**Start polishing yourself today, you will appreciate the changes.**

**Give yourself the conviction to take action.**

**Enjoy the challenge of starting to become the new you.**

# Take action and give yourself more enthusiasm

If there's one product everyone will buy, it's enthusiasm – your most essential basic requirement for success. Without your wholehearted zest and enthusiasm your business will be flat and uninteresting. You may have wonderful ideas, if so you have every right to be full of the joys of spring allowing your enthusiasm to carry you through. I'm accused of being enthusiastic about ordering a cup of coffee, well if it's true, that's fine by me.

As mentioned previously, I bought a run down private school and converted it into a three star hotel. What I didn't tell you was I only had enough money for the deposit. Did having insufficient money put me off trying? Not a bit. I convinced the sellers to lend me – the purchaser – most of the money to buy it. I wanted that school so much, that my enthusiasm convinced them I was a good risk. They were right, I sold my other hotel and paid them back from the proceeds.

Put enthusiasm into everything you do and watch how other people want to do those things with you.

**Enthuse and revel in the excitement you create.**

**Keep your new zest for life – for life.**

# Retrain yourself to increase your determination

It's the person with determination who gets ahead, takes the knocks and still comes back for more, who finishes at the top.

I remember the last, and one of the few times I was depressed. I was twenty-one and getting old, I'd left the RAF and was determined to get a sales job. I attended a number of interviews without success. I remember thinking, "I don't know any salesmen, I've no experience, I'll never get a sales job", things seemed pretty grim. I decided that this was no way to carry on; so I attended as many interviews as I possibly could to learn all I could about 'interviewing for sales positions'. I eventually got my first sales job, by which time I was able to answer the interviewers' questions before they even asked them. I went on to write my first book *Selling Yourself* inspired by this achievement.

If you're determined enough you can definitely get almost anything you want.

**Don't rest on your laurels, keep going.**

**Be determined not to be pushed off course.**

# Confidence

One of the most difficult areas of your character to build on is the confidence you have in yourself. It's obviously very difficult to build true confidence, until you have some proven success behind you. Without that success, you could be in danger of having a false belief in your abilities.

I've always worked on the simple principle that I know my products and myself far better than anyone else does, so I'm therefore entitled to the confidence I show in them. Put another way, if you are not confident in yourself or your products, why should anyone else be.

Some people are naturally more self-confident than others, but we can all become more confident, by knowing our products, customers, competitors and ourselves better. Confidence comes from knowledge. Make a determined effort to increase your knowledge of your chosen field.

Have confidence in your true ability – it's even greater than you could ever imagine and requires only fine tuning.

**Have confidence in yourself and your continually increasing ability.**

# Take pride but don't ever gloat

As you progress, you will be entitled to be proud of yourself and your achievements. I could not help having unbelievably mixed feelings of pride and fear when I drove past my early developments and saw the mixers turning, the builders working and the project taking shape.

The fear came from having to cover all the costs from my own endeavours, but what better motivation is there than wanting to maintain that feeling of pride. I was taking action and things were moving forward and I was proud of my ongoing achievements.

**Keep taking action and moving forward – be proud of yourself for doing it.**

# A genuine friendly
# personality...

**I**s a must to keep your customers and staff in a receptive frame of mind. Show the respect they deserve, work on being pleasant and polite, learn to relax and be friendly. Work at putting people at ease so that you can all look forward to enjoying the future benefits together.

Money can buy your staff's time, but it cannot buy their hearts and minds. This can only be earned through respect and treating your staff as partners in your business. I'd like to think that all staff at HCH, if asked, would see themselves as necessary partners in the business. Hold your staff with the same esteem you reserve for your customers. Then they will all try to look after your customers as you would yourself.

There are two people I recall who affected me to an extent that altered and shaped my attitude and actions when dealing with people.

The first was a nurse at an isolation hospital I twice spent time in. Aged five I had diphtheria, aged seven scarlet fever. An extremely spiteful person, she took a dislike to me, making my miserable stays in hospital far worse. I forced myself to keep a low profile. Being seen but not heard made me less noticeable and less likely to be treated as the butt for her sarcastic, spiteful jibes.

Unfortunately, I adopted a subconscious habit which took me many years to get rid of. I continued this habit when I went back to school. If I didn't understand something, I kept it to myself rather than put myself into the limelight. This resulted in me leaving school with no qualifications or even the ability to do simple arithmetic. I decided never to act in the same way as this nurse, if I did I would deserve it if others treated me the same. Always treat others the way you would like to be treated yourself.

The second – a sales manager, whose weekly sales meetings took the form of verbal abuse and humiliation directed at anyone who had not hit their sales targets. The result of this twice weekly pasting was that all the sales force, successful and not so successful, felt insecure. They were always on the look out for another job. These meetings produced nothing but a high turnover of staff. This manager did not have a clue about how to motivate people, or a sense of common decency. He may well have felt he was frightening his team into producing short term results now and again. Ultimately, all he accomplished was the destruction of any trust and respect from all of his sales force, and a definite loss of future success.

These experiences were real, and I learned from them. I became determined never to have a negative effect on the people I worked with.

**Your personality is your secret weapon.**

**Inspire and lead others for future success.**

**Enrich the lives of others as you progress.**

# Build and improve your analytical mind

Y ou must train yourself to analyse all problems. If you cannot achieve a goal, then you have a problem and the only answer is to come up with a long term solution.

The sales manager in the previous section, would have produced far better results if he'd taken time to think why some people had poor sales – as opposed to jumping up and down looking for a quick fix. He could only think one way. Sales are low = salesmen aren't working hard enough = let's get the whip out.

Analyse your problems by writing them down and breaking them into various headings. Find the real reason why the problem exists – sometimes it is not the obvious cause you first think of. Seek out, change and remove the root cause and the problem will disappear.

Almost any problem can eventually be overcome, if you don't believe me take a look at the Tom Hanks film, Apollo 13. A remarkable true account demonstrating how team effort and analytical thinking can overcome seemingly insurmountable problems.

A problem is like a weed in your garden, you can chop away at the leaves for years and they'll always grow back. Dig out the roots properly, just once, and it's gone for good. It's the same with your business and personal problems – quick fixes are just that, quick fixes, until the next time. Start to take long term actions now.

If your sales are low, and orders are not sufficient, the most common response is to work harder and longer hours making more calls. That response may well work, but if the underlying problem is the companies you are calling on are not big enough to order in sufficient quantities, you can remove the problem by spending more time and effort on larger customers who are able to order larger amounts more regularly. It may initially take more time to accomplish, but if you ignore it, the problem will remain and continue to resurface in the future.

Another very common reason for low sales, which most business people will not readily admit to, is that your potential customers do not know about you.

A planned marketing campaign within the limits of available funds is the key. Use a balanced mix of advertising, personal letters, media publicity (whenever you do something different) and above all else direct contact to ensure your existing and potential customers are consistently reminded of your services. Ensure you provide a satisfactory, dependable service and an excellent product, satisfied customers are the best advertisement you can ever have.

Maybe your product is not quite what your customers want. Spend more time listening to your customers, then change it to meet their demands. Take action to change it now for future success – make their day! Give your customers what they really want.

## Don't just stumble along: Plan your future!

## Ensure you give your customers what they really want.

# Make the most of your personal appearance

**L**et's start with another couple of classic clichés 'you only get one chance at a first impression' and 'you are generally initially accepted as who you appear to be'. Both of which are simple, true and accurate.

Personal appearance is of great importance, especially where success is concerned. So much can depend upon that first impression, do not give yourself an unnecessary disadvantage from the start. Dress and groom yourself as smartly as befits your business and develop an upright and alert presence.

Look alert and successful – guess what? People will start to think you are successful before you really are. None of us like to make silly mistakes, so why should we be the one to buy from a failure?

Make an effort to rid yourself of any annoying mannerisms, ear pulling, lip biting etc., no customer will listen to you properly if you are continually distracting them.

Always improve yourself but never talk down to others.

**Look alive and be successful.**

# Make yourself more interesting through gestures

Get into the habit of backing up what you say with positive gestures. It will provide more emphasis, colour and life to your presentation. Take a look at all the best speakers, live or on TV – what makes them the best is not just what they say, it's the way they deliver it. Your presentation is as important as the content.

**Demonstrate your enthusiasm by your gestures leading others along the way.**

# The hidden you – speech

You can hide your appearance behind a telephone but not your voice, make it presentable. You will be mixing with people of all levels, you must always be at least up to their standard. An accent is not necessarily a disadvantage but coarse speech and slang most certainly are.

As a young lad I had a pronounced Black Country accent. I'm not embarrassed by my roots, in fact I'm rather proud, but it did occur to me that I needed to soften up some parts.

I lost the thickest part of my accent whilst in the RAF by practising and singing the words properly. To use time efficiently and effectively and for privacy this was often in the bath! Eventually becoming barth instead of bath!

**You are generally accepted as what you appear to be.**

# Smile, but make it natural

This obvious action that so many forget to use is a secret weapon and a favourite of mine. There is unbelievable value in a warm genuine smile, it breaks the ice and helps your prospect into a pleasant frame of mind. More, far more than that, it is a true indication that you enjoy what you are doing.

The key is of course a genuine friendly smile, a smile that is bred by genuine excitement, interest and confidence in yourself, your business and your customers' role within it. Forced smiles are easy to spot, they disappear very soon.

It's going to take more than this book to put a genuine smile on the face of someone who's doing something they don't enjoy. If you have to regularly fake a smile, take a long look at what you're doing. If you can't change it sufficiently to put that smile back, look for something else that can, it's that important.

I am told that I constantly have a smile on my face. I wouldn't know, I'm too happy doing what I'm doing to notice it.

**Be happy, smile and influence others.**

# The Value of a Smile

Smiling is infectious,
You catch it like the flu,
When someone smiled at me today,
I started smiling too!

I walked around a corner,
And someone saw my grin,
When he smiled too I realised,
I'd passed it onto him.

I thought about this smile of mine,
and realised what it's worth,
A single smile began by me,
Could travel round the earth!

So if you feel your smile begin,
Don't leave it undetected,
Let's start an epidemic now,
and get the world infected!

# Conversation

The true art of conversation, is to be a good listener, listening with genuine interest. The true art of listening is in understanding. It's the same when you're reading. It's not good enough to just see the words, you have to absorb, analyse and apply, we come across so many people who take this advice at face value, instead of genuinely understanding.

They sit and listen, in fact they go overboard and hardly contribute to the conversation, which ends up flat and boring. The words go in one ear – as they hold themselves back from speaking – and the words go out the other, as they bite their lip to stop interrupting. All their concentration is focused on stopping themselves talking, as opposed to genuinely trying to understand. Show your interest, add to and draw out what the other person is saying.

Take time to genuinely understand the other person. Prove you are listening and understanding their aspirations and you will have the most important information that you need to converse with them. Have your fair share of the discussion, contribute to it by asking questions about the other person's problems or wishes, but don't hog all of the limelight.

Understanding comes from listening and observing how the speaker delivers key points via emphasis and gestures.

Ultimately you understand someone through their continual actions, not just their words. If they don't give you that order, or deliver on a promise, you'd better listen and understand that. Actions truly speak louder than words and don't ever let anyone convince you otherwise.

Show genuine interest through the questions you ask. Most people are genuinely more interested in talking about themselves and their desires, than listening to yours.

**Be an interested listener.**

# Your future depends on controlled conversation

**L**earn to lead important conversations the way you want them to go. Do not ever lose track of your original intentions. Always come back to your planned sequence of discussion.

Controlling a conversation is achieved by preparation. Know exactly what you want to achieve and the stages you need to go through. Take time out to genuinely answer any queries or objections as they arise. Confirm the answers are satisfactory before moving back to your planned approach. To direct a rambling conversation back to your agenda, ask a question that will take you there.

**Plan your future aims then lead others with you.**

# Keep an open mind and always be prepared to accept constructive criticism

Another golden oldie – 'you're never too old or too experienced to learn something new'. No matter how long you have been in your business, you must always be willing to listen and learn. Wherever possible learn by and take advantage of other people's mistakes instead of making your own.

It's up to you to decide whether to follow their criticism, adapt it, utilise it or forget it. Decide if their criticism makes sense, if it does, take action and make a change for the better now.

The key is in understanding and analysing constructive criticism and advice when it's given. All too often, people find their way back to the same old problems, treading water instead of moving on. Make a commitment to really learn from your own and others' bright ideas. Put in a plan of action to ensure you don't make the mistake of missing them again.

Show appreciation and follow the best decision or planned route, whoever thought of it. Think it through, adjust, adapt and amend it until it is right and then take action. Be in the forefront of your market by being your own best critic and ensure you learn from your own potential mistakes. Hopefully before you make them. Take action and, if necessary, change course now for the better.

Be aware that not all advice and criticism will be constructive. Some people do not know how to give it, others will take pleasure in knocking you at every opportunity. In the long run you'd be better off avoiding these sort of people. In the meantime, use your own judgement as to their value. Have a thick skin and don't be put off course by false advice or petty jealous criticism

My neighbours on my Council Estate were well aware of my first venture, a five ton van does make an impact! They started to queue, even before my coal-fired fryers were hot enough to cook in. I dressed the part with my cravat, white jacket, black trousers and boots.

On the opening night of my fish and chip business, I had pretested cooking beautiful golden chips in palm kernel oil. Due to the cost, I had not bothered to pre-test with fish. Unfortunately no-one explained that you had to coat the fish with flour to make the batter stick. I failed to carry out this simple action. The first customers in the queue confirmed that this meant fish at one end of the fryer and batter at the other!

An unfortunate, expensive and very fast way to learn. It was like being on stage without rehearsing my lines – exciting but confusing.

The coal fires eventually heated on a regular basis and my business life began. There were few safety devices in those days. I had to put in a full batch of uncooked chips, then drive like mad to my next venue. Once the chips were cooked, unless I needed more, the only way to cool the fat was to throw water in and quickly shut the lids, to the accompaniment of big bangs as the fat exploded!

The 12 inch metal venting chimney came out of and up the outside of the van without any protective covering – people sometimes swore if they accidentally touched it.

No thoughts of suing in those days. It was considered their own fault for not watching what they were doing.

**Do not be afraid to admit your shortfalls – but take quick action to change them.**

**Look on problems as a challenge and an opportunity – a test for your new abilities.**

# Direct yourself forward by planning ahead

It is essential to have a good plan before taking action. A plan is the essential tool for efficiency, optimum use of time and stress relief. Analyse your ambitions, where you want to go and decide what you intend to achieve. Have a definite goal for inspiration. Work out, through your plan, what path you will have to take and when you will have to take it.

Once your plan is in place, take action one chapter at a time. Follow your plan on a day to day basis, hit the deadlines you set and discipline yourself always to do today, what you used to put off until tomorrow.

Continually update and re-balance your plan and it will deliver for you.

**Follow your action plan step by step.**

# Have an open mind and see the other person's point of view

The difficulty here is how to do it. Most of us try to see the other person's point of view through our own perceptions. In this situation, what most of us see is what we would do in their position, which is often different from what they would do.

Always, when selling yourself or your product, revolve your sales story around how it will help your customer. How it will benefit them is the most important factor in their eyes. How it will make them feel better or look better? Financially is usually the prime appeal, how much extra profit? You can also appeal to vanity, personal pride or business sense, every person has their soft spot. Note your customers' reactions until you hit the right one for them.

**Make their day, give them what they want.**

# Criticism or Complaints

S hould of course always to be treated seriously, but also fairly. A two-way opportunity to solve and rectify the situation, they should be made fairly and nicely as soon as possible after the incident. Giving the person who made the mistake, the opportunity to quickly rectify it. Show tolerance to others, it may even be their first day at the job (then appreciate their problem solving efforts with a smile). People who feel annoyed without saying anything until they tell a cashier, when leaving three days later, give no opportunity to make amends.

You cannot change the past, but you can influence the future. Forgive and forget, do not let any accidental incidents spoil your day, always give a welcoming thank you as it is put right! Sometimes perceived expectations make some people more sensitive than normal. If you do keep getting similar complaints, you obviously need to act quickly to change and permanently resolve them.

If over 95% of your customers are happy and the others keep offering different complaints it could be simply accidental, "No one's perfect all the time". Do your best to solve it to the extent of the problem but beware and do not capitulate to people who simply want unfair discounts. Don't give in to bullying tactics and don't let them bully your nice staff.

Providing you are always striving to keep your customers

happy and your staff committed and enthusiastic, you are on
the right track.

# Take care of yourself and keep your finest asset in top working order

**W**hat would happen to your car if you didn't change the oil, clean off the dirt and have regular services? Yes, we all know that eventually it'll rust away or the engine will blow up. As this could take years to happen, missing an oil change here or a clean there doesn't really matter, right? Wrong, neglect, any personal neglect will affect top performance and your future success.

Keep yourself as fit and healthy as possible. It will help reduce your stress. Stretching, press-ups and simple muscle toning exercises, especially ten minutes before breakfast will not take long but will pay constant dividends. Gym work three or four times a week, would be even better still. If you feel better you look better, looking better makes you feel better. Drink at least one litre of water each day, this will detoxify your body.

You are what you think! As well as what you eat!

Learn to enjoy short periods of rest and relaxation as part of your planned way forward. All things in moderation, intertwined with enjoyable excesses of work and play will contribute to a fuller, healthier and happier life.

Don't worry, it's non-productive! But always show lots of concern.

If you get too stressed and uptight, here are a couple of techniques that work for me. Sit quietly for two minutes, hands on stomach, breathe in slowly and deeply from the stomach, hold for a count of five. Breathe out slowly and hold for five whilst clearing your mind. Then, concentrate on relaxing each part of your body starting with your feet moving up to your ankles, calves, knees, thighs etc., counting down from 20 as you concentrate on relaxing each area. Give your mind and body a few minutes to rebuild. Alternatively get up and take a short walk or change what you're doing for something else, coming back to your problem area later.

The **Placebo Effect** - feel good and happy and your mind and body feels better.

## Be a happy optimist. Make music play in your life and in the lives of others.

# Enjoy and progress by not wasting your time but making the most of it

We all need periods of relaxation, a switch-off to recharge mind and body for the business challenges of the next day. Effective relaxation time is as important to your plan as effective work time. Give yourself a reward, something to regularly look forward to. The danger lies in distinguishing between relaxation and procrastination. It's all too easy to excuse one for the other.

Look at how you use your relaxation time in relation to how badly you want success. Does sitting in front of the TV watching Coronation Street really contribute to your life? It could be that you enjoy and need the switch off it gives you.

Make changes to what you do with your time, use it to contribute to your overall plans. Balance your relaxation time properly with your family or partner, according to your own and your family's needs. Make sure that they are aware that they will also share the benefits of your success. Set reward goals that include them, let their enthusiasm join with yours.

You have to be prepared for change – how much do you really want success and what degree of success do you really want? Change your habits to use time constructively, remembering we all aspire to different things and have differing ideals for success and relaxation. Know yourself, be honest with yourself, always build good foundations for the future and make certain you do what you have to do today.

I recently had a conversation where the other person said they would like a fortnight's holiday on a small boat tracking whales. That's fine for them, but not for me. To enjoy myself and wind down, I would need to use my time doing something else. Choose the type of relaxation you need.

**Relax, but always do whatever it takes today and everyday to keep your business on a successful course.**

**Remember, you are working hard now to improve your future lifestyle.**

**Reward yourself for your successes.**

**The Way you Live will eventually become your Way of Life.**

# A little on time management

I was recently asked what sort of time management tools and techniques I use. "Oh, I'm basic at it really, I trained myself to carry a pen and pad with me all the time to jot down ideas and remind myself of tasks. I also keep it beside my bed to note down ideas as they come to me. Then I can go to sleep again."

You're practising the number one habit. was the questioner's reply.

There are plenty of modern time management aids available, I find that a well planned diary, my note pad and my anti-worry book (more about that later) do the job well for me. Ensure you don't forget your best ideas and use whatever works best for you to make every minute count.

**Don't just progress by accident, do it with intent.**

**Enjoy every moment of your actions.**

**See the future creating itself
thanks to your own day-to-day actions.**

# Make the most of your assets

**T**he greatest natural assets you have are the characteristics outlined in previous pages. Polish them, change them, make working on them a habit and they will become a natural part of your personality in your business and social life. After all, a business person never knows when a casual acquaintance will turn into a mutually beneficial prospect.

Genuine sincerity comes from belief and conviction. Initially you may feel as if it's all an act but concentrate upon changing your habits, have the conviction to stay with the changes and maintain belief. You will ultimately develop the characteristics of a successful person, in time they will become a natural part of you and your future success.

Ensure that you always treat other people the way you would like to be treated yourself.

If you act successful, look successful, think successful, talk successful – you will definitely be more successful.

**Success breeds success.**

# Wave that magic wand

How would you like proof that you can change for the better by changing one of the habits that's been holding you back?

Take action now in one area of your life. What about making those phone calls you've been putting off? Writing that plan you've been promising to do? Keeping your forward planning diary up to date, making more effective use of your work time, dealing with that niggling problem that won't go away or maybe even giving up smoking, eating a healthier diet, starting to exercise on a regular basis, less time down the pub?

Decide what actions you need to take, commit yourself to doing it, see yourself doing it and start doing it now.

Prove to yourself that you can make a change, that you can make something happen and you'll be amazed when you do and by what you can do.

Make the decision, do it, stick with it, take control of your decisions and do not go back to your old habits. Feel the power of your decisions and understand that you can control what you do. It's only your decision to do otherwise that will stop your progress.

You can decide to make that call or you can decide not to; you can decide to make every minute count or you can decide to procrastinate; you can decide to spend more quality time with your family or you can decide to do something else – you're lucky, you can control your future. But be fair to yourself, don't punish yourself just for fun, when making changes make sure it's a worthwhile action.

You have a tremendous advantage over the person who only thinks they would like to be successful and is vaguely attempting to do so. You know what you have to do. You can see that it's taking control of your decisions and taking action that makes the difference. Create an action plan – then action it!

Start right now, do not accept that it might not work, you now know different. The only reason it will not work is if you decide it won't.

Start now and build other people's enthusiasm with your own. You're on your way to future success

**You can control what you do.**

**Take a worthwhile action now.**

**Feel enthusiastic about your future, you are making things happen, feel great about it.**

# Section Two – You And Your Business

# Applying Yourself to Find a Successful Business Opportunity

**M**ost would-be entrepreneurs find this to be their most frequent stumbling block. But really, it s not so difficult, put your background, knowledge, interests and hobbies to the test.

The big difference is being able to distinguish between what's just a good idea and what's a good potential business project. There are many excellent ideas that at face value seem unbelievable opportunities. Unfortunately, just because they are excellent ideas does not mean they will translate into profitable businesses.

I mentioned earlier that one of my first business ventures was an 'introduction agency'. At the time they were almost unheard of, and with national service in operation my idea was – lots of young single men leaving national service, plenty of young single women looking for them – let's put them together. Nothing wrong with the idea, but lots wrong with the business behind the idea.

It was ahead of its time, men would register, but women felt it too forward or pushy. In addition, my marketing attempts were stifled by newspapers not accepting my adverts obviously thinking I was into something a little more seedy than I was. It's easy to make a mistake like this, make sure you don't, discipline yourself to be totally honest in your personal assessment of your opportunity.

1. Are you totally committed to making it work? Do you have the necessary skills? Start making notes again now.

2. What alternatives do your potential customers currently have? Can you offer better?

3. Do you know what all your costs and overheads are likely to be? Whatever costs you anticipate, there will always be more you haven't thought about. Put in a further 10% contingency.

4. What could be the most likely causes of failure? Can you overcome them?

5. Can you honestly make a profit from the venture? Do your figures add up? Re- check them.

6. Do you have enough cash to stay in business during the development stages?

7. Does your business conform to legal and statutory requirements?

Starting a business, like getting married or buying a new house, is an unbelievably exciting event and possibly frightening. Emotions and expectations, if allowed, can run wild. The first business skill required is to be able to distinguish between what is wishful thinking and what is realistically achievable. It's the art of keeping your feet on the ground whilst all the time remaining optimistic and enthusiastic. No that's not a contradiction, it's what you have to do.

Most business failures are for one of two main reasons;

1.   Lack of profit.
2.   Lack of cash.

There are many reasons why a company doesn't make a profit – bad management, poor sales, high overheads, bad planning, bad debts – but in the end it's lack of cash through lack of profits that finishes a business.

Never forget, even conveniently, that profit eventually means cash in and a loss means cash out. Those fortunate enough to start a positive cash flow business, need to constantly remind themselves of this reality – if after your initial build up period you're still consistently making a loss, you're going out of business, unless you change your plan and begin to show positive profitable results.

**Think it through before you do it.
Use your own hidden talents continually.**

# Are you totally committed? Do you have the necessary skills?

Ask yourself the following questions and write down your answers:-

1. Why do you want to be successful?

2. Are you willing to make sacrifices?

3. Why do you think your idea could sell?

4. What steps have you taken to back up and prove your assumptions?

5. What do you know about your competitors and their products?

6. What do you know about your competitors' future ideas?

7. What are your main interests?

8. Do these fit into your business aims?

9. What are your ambitions?

10. What do you think are the basic qualifications for achieving your ambitions – do you possess them?

11. Are you fully aware of the commitment required to achieve your ambitions and the sacrifices you will have to make?

12. Can your personal life cope with the demands of your ambitions?

13. How will you enjoy your future success?

Your replies must reflect your personality and potential. You must answer honestly. To be forewarned is to be forearmed, analyse your answers – do they still give you a favourable impression? If not, work on any weaknesses and prepare to change them.

The first two questions listed are the most important. If your answers show a total enthusiasm and commitment for your project then you can make it work – providing you've done your homework and continue to live with your plan, making whatever sacrifices are necessary to make it come true.

Constantly analyse, update and improve yourself. Operating your own business will offer far more variety, but will require constant daily hard earned results. When you start off, you are the business, it has no life of its own with no easy repeat orders, you have to continually guide and lead it along.

A successful business person must be prepared to keep going, putting more and more life into the business through constant effort. Your business will eventually develop a life of its own. It will generate continued future business from its goodwill and customer awareness.

You will see this happening as you progress, take satisfaction that your efforts are being rewarded, but don't slip into a false sense of security. A business not adapting and moving forward is a business going out of business, your competitors will make sure of that.

Initially you must concentrate upon building a firm foundation. Your immediate target is not to be top, that comes later, but to be successful at each stage, the first and most important phase is passing break-even into profit. Ensure your overheads and spending are as low as possible – do not try to run before you can walk.

Long term success and survival will depend upon your company having a quality product. It may even be slightly higher priced than your competitors' and may take a little longer to establish but it will pay off in the long run. Make use of your previous experience and up to date analysis to operate a better quality business than your competitors.

Never enter into a business until you have fully analysed it and are sure of your ability to make a success of it. It is far better to be successful on a small scale than to be a failure in a business you are not yet ready for.

Make your business your favourite hobby, your success will then be even more rewarding and enjoyable.

**Think deeply now rather than despair later.**

**Concentrate on success at each and every stage.**

**Plan purposely and progress steadily.**

**Make your business your favourite hobby!**

# Appreciate life and learn to relax and enjoy the more menial jobs

I n the early stages of business, many make the usually fatal mistake of increasing overheads in line with their inflated forecasts. Don't fool yourself, don't spend it until you've earned it.

Carefully check and decide the necessity for every capital expenditure you are thinking of making. Do you need that new van yet? Also every additional overhead – do you really need a larger office or workshop yet? Keep up this policy forever. Adding these extra overheads now could spoil your future.

It's a satisfying aspect of business that you can employ people and provide work within a community. But employ people for the right reasons and not just because you want to be a boss or you want 'others' to do the work for you.

Learn to enjoy the more menial jobs, see them as part of the way to success. You'll be thankful you've not taken on more staff when you hit a tough patch (and you will have them) and cash is at a premium.

**Take consolidating action one step at a time.**

# You as an employer

**A**lways think in terms of long term team building and always employ the best people you can. If you need a centre forward don't employ the best goalkeeper, wait until you come across a centre forward or at least a good potential centre forward.

In the mid-sixties it was extremely difficult to recruit willing staff, twice I had to go to Majorca to obtain experienced waiters who wanted to learn English and were willing to work. At that time I would serve drinks in the bar, wait at tables in the restaurant, act as a chauffeur for the cleaning staff whatever it took. But when I employed staff I would always ensure they were able to do their own job to the standard my customers expected of me.

My role was to develop and continually maintain a good atmosphere and team spirit. A team always performs when its members have confidence in each other. When they can trust each other to perform in a quality way consistently. Always motivate, show your staff the way you want them to go, convince them of the benefits of team work and make it your job to keep the team spirit alive. Create a charm school for your staff by setting the perfect example.

Always delegate to people able to work as well as yourself but never, under any circumstances, delegate what should be your responsibility. Remember you're in charge and will have to pick up any pieces that fall apart. Always make the final decision in areas that can critically affect your business. Even today at HCH I talk things through with my team but retain control and responsibility over all policy decisions, pricing and capital expenditure. No one makes any changes without my agreement!

I have been asked why I don't allow my senior staff to make these decisions, after all it's what most text books will tell you. The answer is I must always be in control of the overall blueprint of my present and future aims. It's worked for me in the past and continues to work well for me now. It would be unfair to give ultimate responsibility for the company's future to others. Thankfully I do enjoy the hands-on feel that comes with it.

There will come a time when you'll have to hand over the reigns. Someone will need to fill the vacuum left when you decide to retire or go to that big heaven in the sky. "Now there's a challenge!" Your long term aim is to identify those people and bring them further and further into the business, teaching them to take actions that you, as the overall planner, would approve of.

Work as a team but be a benevolent dictator and a jolly good team leader.

### You are responsible for your future success.

# How to keep staff and get the best out of them

- Lead and motivate your essential back-up team.

- Make sure your staff enjoy the work as much as possible by creating a friendly happy atmosphere to work in.

- Make your business the best and most satisfying place they could work in.

- Make sure you don't employ disruptive people or those who spend time playing office politics – both sorts create bad atmospheres.

- Always show appreciation when it's due.

- Try to employ only nice people that you like and feel safe with.

- Prove that you don't want to cheat your staff by making them aware of how well the business is doing and paying a fair salary.

- Incentivise and share your success with your management and staff.

- Make sure your staff are aware of their potential future – they need their own goals to aim for – and reward for good performance.

- Set fair targets and success related bonuses.

- Never back down on a promise of promotion, unless there is a most compelling reason.

- Make all major decisions after listening to your staff.

- Appreciating your staff and their skills will balance yours. Ensure they do better as you do.

**Work as a team and progress together.**

# Why will people buy from you?

**P**eople buy to fulfil a need, in business this usually translates to profit, success and satisfaction. To satisfy that need you must know your product and understand exactly how it benefits your customer. Know your competitors, their quality, price, design, advertising, distribution – everything you can. Doing so will highlight where you can offer more.

Know what it is that attracts customers to your competitor's business – then do it better based on the customers' known requirements. Find the weaknesses in your competitors' service and make them your strengths and a focus of your sales policy and presentation.

Your potential customers are looking for a company that will provide reliable backing in their mission for profits, success and a satisfactory service.

Find out:

1. How well your potential customers are doing.

2. Who your competitors are – big and small – who is the most successful and why? Is it quality, service or price?

3. What degree of advertising they undertake.

4. What marketing material they use. Obtain leaflets, price lists and any other relevant information. Potential competitors often phone HCH asking for sales literature. Some go as far as telling me they are looking to open a health spa and ask how can they make it successful!

You have your competitors' background. Analyse them, see what their aims are and their strengths and weaknesses. Aim at their weaknesses. Make yourself and your business or product as good as you possibly can by exploiting their weaknesses.

Aim for long term success by satisfying your customers' needs. Financial success will follow – you can't be successful in business without making money.

**Applied knowledge is power.**

**Guide yourself not your competitors.**

**Think hard about it – you eventually become what you think about.**

# How to sell yourself and your products

First of all let's get things into perspective. You may want success, but make no mistake, it's of little interest to your potential customers. Look for a niche in the market, something that is going to make you different from what is already available. What do you want that you have difficulty finding?

As a general rule don't go looking for the one-off opportunity. If there is a genuine demand and therefore a genuine business opportunity, ask yourself why someone else isn't doing it already? Is it a good or even excellent idea, yet a lousy business opportunity? Being the 'first' presents huge marketing and customer awareness problems. Trying to inform a market of a new product or service that they have never used before can be mighty expensive and time consuming– do you have that sort of budget?

You're better off doing what you are good at. Do something that other people do and make money from – but do it better! There are no prizes for being a 'pioneer' in business, the only prizes come from staying in business and that means making a profit.

You must actively sell yourself and your product's benefits.

The best and only real sales are when customers, after listening to your presentation, decide they need your product.

Undoubtedly some sales are made through pressure tactics. But don't expect to get second or subsequent orders. Unless your customers have bought because they recognise the benefits to them through your presentation, you have not done a good job for the future.

The continued success of your business is through your customers deriving a genuine and measurable benefit from your product and not from high pressure selling or false claims. If your product does not deliver a benefit, it's only a matter of time before your customers and the industry you work in realise you have nothing of significant value to offer.

Find out what your customer needs – offer it in a pleasant, confident and honest presentation.

As stated previously, a customer is looking for a product that is going to be of genuine value to satisfy their need. Your role is to convince them by showing and proving you can satisfy that need.

**Plan your sales approach, don't just sell the sausage sell the sizzle.**

**Give service and quality.**

# Have you done your homework? Have you written it down to clarify your aims? You must!

# Do you know what the majority of your costs and overheads are likely to be?

# Honestly, do you really think you can make a profit?

**M**any business people have overestimated initial sales and underestimated the costs. The excitement of starting a new business and basing sales on expectations fuelled by the overwhelming desire to succeed, often translates into unrealistic sales forecasts.

Be aware of this, by all means do a plan of what you would like to happen and work at achieving it. More importantly, search for the reality of what will happen in the beginning and decide if it's a business idea with a viable long term future

Is there truly sufficient demand? Can you capture enough orders at the right price to generate sufficient profits? When forecasting sales take into account your competitors. They will not always take your entry into the market sitting down, they will react to you. How could this affect your forecast? What effect will it have if they reduce their prices? Be optimistic but don't underestimate your future costs.

1. Carefully pre-check your potential customers also the appropriate location that will appeal to them. My café was on a busy road, but on the wrong side. The bus terminus and most of the pedestrians were on the other side. I made more profit from selling than operating it. Luckily the purchaser was also unaware of this simple fact.

2. Cost the project – What is the gross profit? This is the difference between the direct costs of products and your sale price. Be realistic – under current market conditions, what price and gross profit can you expect? Again, there are normally two figures, what you would like and what you'll get – be a realistic optimist.

3. What is your monthly break-even figure? Add your profit margin per item or per day etc. What is your potential monthly gross profit? Deduct monthly overheads i.e. rent or finance charges, rates, heating, stationery, lighting, staff costs etc. not forgetting what you need. (You need a minimum income to live on, what is it? Better still, if possible, keep your existing income by working part-time

until your business can support you. You need to keep the wolves from the door. If you don't, this can make for unforeseen problems at home.) Can they all be covered?

Running your own business means you're effectively working on a **commission-only basis**. Pay yourself more than your business earns and if you want to stay in business, you'll have to pay it back – generally by incurring more debt.

If your normal profit potential is less than your total costs and you don't have sufficient capital to survive until it becomes profitable, choose a different business or wait until you have enough capital.

### Fact finding saves funds.

### Cost your product and your minimum basic overheads.

### Your personal income will be on a commission (results) only basis.

# Do you have enough cash to stay in business?

**L**ack of cash to pay your way is generally the biggest problem encountered in a new business. Overestimated profit and sales forecasts, result in underestimated cash requirements and a negative cash flow.

Very few businesses start up and progress without the need for external financing. Understanding your finances and the types of finance available are critical for obtaining support.

You will require seed capital, asset finance and working capital. Knowing the difference and how banks work, can make the difference between raising funds or not.

Even if they'd like us to believe differently, banks are not in the business of lending unsecured capital to new businesses. It's like trying to buy a new car at a fruit and veg. stall – they don't sell new cars.

Understanding your financial requirements and the different forms of finance available, is a complex area which would be above a book of this nature. Working out your potential take and your estimated overheads to produce a cash flow forecast for the first two years is your first move. The advice is to then get advice.

Keep going to see the bank for advice or trial presentations until you know how they would like the plan presented. Remember, I went to enough sales interviews to enable me to know the questions (and answers) before they were raised. Be prepared to be asked for personal guarantees and some form of loan security. Banks are not charities, they exist to make profits by lending money and not letting go of the money they already have.

Prove that you know what you're talking about and prove that you understand your business' potential finances, through a well presented business plan.

It's important to point out that a business plan is your plan of action. It's not worth the paper it's written on unless the plan is realistic and you have every intention and possibility of hitting targets staying within budgets and time scales.

Some, it has to be said, see a business plan solely as a vehicle for raising money, discarding it the moment the money's in their bank. The plan must be your statement of intent, you will have to prove its credibility. Your performance, when measured against the plan, is a true reflection of your understanding of the business and your commitment to becoming successful.

To retain credibility you would need to explain differences between actual results and forecast figures. Differences will occur, I've yet to see a business plan that's been spot on, but they will need to be explained satisfactorily. If you can't, why else should anyone continue to support and respect you or believe your next stage plan or idea?

Set realistic targets, hit your targets, deliver on your plans, prove that you are a stayer who will not collapse under the pressure and raising funds for future expansion will be a lot easier.

Do not try to start at the top with high borrowing and overheads, practise and plan with the lowest possible overheads until you are sure of your product's potential success.

It may not sound as exciting, but if you can manage to keep your normal job whilst you consolidate your ideas, so much the better.

Prove the viability of your enterprise before investing and risking large sums of finance. Start small and teach yourself vital business skills on a shoestring – prove your ability before trying to borrow larger sums, you then have a practical background to offer. It will be quicker and less painful in the long run.

Early in my career, I kept a successful day-job that provided a salary and company car, enabling me to finance the initial hotel developments that were my evening and weekend work. Admittedly, my daily way of life was nearly all work, but

I enjoyed most of it! In reality, I had no alternative! Commitment and action following a workable plan will eventually pay dividends.

One last word on cash – in my experience any major expansion has always been followed by a strain on cash flow. More business generated generally means higher overheads which may have to be paid before you receive cash from the extra sales. Additionally, your suppliers will still want their money on time. It may be worth talking your plans through with a few major suppliers who will benefit from your expansion. They may agree an extended credit period to help with the expansion but they will probably want a contract for the future business. Agreed trade credit, (paying particular attention to the word agreed) is the cheapest form of finance available but you have to be realistic and stick to the agreed terms.

## Keep your costs as low as possible.

## Work within your cash flow raising finance only when you are capable of proving your ability to service your debt.

# Recognise and solve your own problems

**A** problem is anything which gets in your way and stops you from following your plans. Most people get bogged down with problems without fully realising what their problems really are!

The inability to cope with problems could easily make us depressed! It's up to you to deal with problems efficiently, as one thing's for sure, they're going to keep coming along – it's supposed to be part of the fun of being in business.

How you view problems will effect the way you deal with them. I have a tendency to enjoy problems – well, the satisfaction of sorting out a solution at least. Instead of being non-productive and worrying, analyse the full situation. You know what you want, what you are doing, why you are doing it – what's stopping you from achieving? Write it down and clarify it. Then you can decide the best actions to solve it.

By dealing with a problem in this way, you have the advantage. You are the expert on yourself and your business plans, so what can you do to change your situation? Work within the framework of your objective – but constantly fine-tune and upgrade your aims. Making steady progress at alleviating a problem might be slower, but it's better than a short flash-in-the-pan solution that cannot be sustained.

Your first step is to establish what the real problem is? Always remember that it may not be apparent at first. The effect can very often hide the true cause. By writing down the problem and analysing it, you change the problem from being a worry that you may not be able to cope with, into a smaller set of faults that you can.

My own way of doing this is through what I call my anti-worry book. It's a book – I'm probably on my 30th – I've kept in my top drawer for over 30 years. I make notes, when I need to, of the day and date of the biggest worry I have. As I write down and analyse the problem, I break it down into issues and investigate all the possible causes. I isolate the faults I can deal with immediately and take action, starting with the easiest As I move on to the more difficult, I look for alternative ways of eliminating, or if that's not possible, changing the issue to where I can gain an advantage.

Consider delaying actions that can immediately stop the problem from getting worse, when you make a change ensure it's a worthwhile one. Most problems come down to a lack of funds, staff training, pricing, service or quality standards, or even success above your organisation's ability to cope with it, ensure you make real changes for a better future.

Either way I have found my book serves its purpose, once a problem is written down and analysed I am able to get on with other tasks instead of spending time worrying. It clears my mind and helps me find alternative solutions and opportunities. In addition, it acts as a fine reference to my feelings on, and immediate gut reactions to, problems and how I dealt with them.

**Make sure you fully understand your problems before you start to change them.**

**Act to rectify all known problems as soon as possible.**

**Change and adapt to stop them reoccurring.**

**Don't turn a small calamity into a large crisis.**

# What do you do when the solution still doesn't work?

**L**ook back at the steps you have taken, be honest – have you really put in the effort and made genuine progress along the planned route or are you simply not following your initial plan?

Think carefully, write down what areas you feel you are failing in and what steps are needed to rectify the situation now and for the future. Do you still believe you can be a success? Fine, take action.

I also make a few notes in my anti-worry book when I get some exceptional results or good news – a nice pick me up that works in the opposite way to a worry.

**Don't just worry about it – do something.**

# What do you do on the day you feel down?

We're all susceptible to the odd off-day. The first thing to establish is what's causing it. Are you genuinely ill or tired, or are your worries and problems getting you down?

Sometimes disappointment and frustration can lead to dissatisfaction because you have not yet achieved your end result. We all want success to happen overnight, but of course it cannot – success is a continual way of life and not an instant action.

Take a positive look at what you have achieved and trust your own judgement as to whether your commitment and actions are going to plan. If they are, congratulate yourself, your mind and body will appreciate the thanks and give you more power to get started. The most important state of mind is not to wish for or regret, what you do not or cannot have, but to appreciate your achievements and feel content.

If you are genuinely unwell or overtired, take time-out to recharge your batteries, start again when you feel stronger, but do not let this become a false excuse. Physical problems will affect your performance and, more importantly, your future health. Do not avoid them, deal with them.

If your problems are getting on top of you, don't spend too long feeling sorry for yourself, you don't have the time. There is genuinely only one way to start feeling better and that's by taking control of your problems and dealing with them one by one. It's such a great feeling to finally get rid of a problem, even a small one, that it gives an automatic pick up.

Even a day when you're feeling down can be another step towards your future success. Make the extra effort to achieve – a day that starts off badly is a wonderful opportunity to prove to yourself how capable you are and provides the perfect opportunity to change your attitude to life!

Even on a bad day you should be thankful that your future is in your own hands – others may seem to be influencing it, but you are still in control of your options and destiny. You make the choice on whether you lie down, sit down or stand up straight. Whatever action you take will have a profound effect on what happens to your day and your well being.

If in doubt about what to do, write down your options. It will clear and start to cleanse the mind. Force yourself to take action with the most favourable option, your motivation levels will increase through your own effort and action. It's true, a bad day stops being a bad day when you turn it into a good day!

On a lighter note, I'm a firm believer that nature makes us feel less lively, happy and enthusiastic now and again. Until you are through this minor phase, relax and enjoy the unusual experience of standing still. If you're committed to success, you'll tire of it soon enough. Had enough? Now start moving.

**A bad day stops being a bad day when you turn it into a good day.**

**Take a positive look at what you've achieved and congratulate yourself**

**Don't get depressed, it's non-productive.**

**Be positive – Take action.**

# Selling

It may seem to be heralded as an over important part of a business person's lot – but selling is the key to your success.

Whether you own a tea shop, garage or manufacturing business, your products and services will not be utilised properly unless you continually market and sell them to your potential customers.

Always soft-sell the benefits. Always make your customers want to buy from you.

## Button up the benefits.

Repeat each benefit in your soft-sell approach

Confirm the benefits again – quality, price, delivery, service, reliability, etc.

Close the sale by getting a nod of the head – confirmation that they understand, agree and appreciate the benefits.

Demonstrate use and value, make them aware of their future satisfaction.

Take Action

Selling is the actions you take that makes your potential customers want to buy your products. Extol its virtues softly but continually.

Sell for now and for the future – make a joint agreement for your next appointment.

Selling yourself, your company and your products and services is a non-stop, action-packed way of life. Every moment opens up a new and exciting opportunity. Revel in it. Enjoy promoting a more successful future for yourself and your team. "What a wonderful life".

**Enjoy what you do and do it with enjoyment.**

**Appreciate the excitement of your progress.**

# What about your suppliers?

We've spent time talking about staff and customers, but let's not forget suppliers. Without good, reliable suppliers that take an interest in the success of your business, you will not perform at your top level.

You can learn a lot about selling by studying why you buy from a certain supplier. Some will no doubt be on price, but I bet your top suppliers, the ones you have the best relationships with, provide far more than just a low price. In fact, they probably don't always give the lowest price available. The best suppliers always provide a combination of price, reliability, consistency, dependability, quality and make an effort to understand your business so they can help you as much as possible and keep your custom. Isn't that how you should be treating your customers?

Building a two way confidence can be a great asset if you ever run into difficulties or short term cash flow problems. A good supplier will want to help you and can provide a lifeline you would not be able to get elsewhere – but only if you have built the relationship on trust and respect.

Treat your suppliers with respect and look for **quality**,

reliability and service at a fair cost. Squeeze their prices by all means, use judgement based on your knowledge of what is a fair price, but expect to leave a little profit for everyone.

It is still my policy to obtain at least two quotes on new products, it makes me more aware of the market and the difference still sometimes amazes me. Give your favourite supplier the chance to match the best offer, always bearing in mind a 'fair price'. Remind yourself how you feel when a customer tries to screw you into the ground and the difference when a customer treats you fairly and respectfully. Which one would you be more inclined to go out of your way to help?

My experiences have taught me to be a good guesser, enabling me to generally follow my gut instincts. Experience will do the same for you.

When possible, make a habit of paying your suppliers on a regular pattern even if it is a month later than they would prefer. Again, turn it the other way, I'm sure you'd prefer to have a customer that pays you consistently and regularly than erratically.

If a supplier makes a mistake, use your judgement to distinguish between incompetence or just a mistake. Allow them to make amends quickly without spoiling a good future relationship.

It's better to have a fair and realistic reaction to a late delivery, than to take any action that will not help the present situation and potentially harm your future relationship. Be as fair and understanding as is reasonable.

Don't make a big issue out of something small going wrong. "In life it often does". See the situation from both points of view:- If it's an unusual, error try to see the funny side and laugh about it together.

Judge your supplier by their response, it's a good way of telling their real worth. Once again, actions speak far louder than words.

## Help your suppliers to help you.

## Work together to help yourself.

# Market yourself, your company and your products at every opportunity

**T**ake advantage of each and every opportunity to show your customers what you can do keeping your name in front of them as often as you can. 'Look for the big cream van with that irresistible aroma calling at ......... on .......', read the promotional leaflets that I pushed through letter boxes on my proposed fish and chip van round.

Even a fish and chip van can be marketed to produce higher sales. I bought my van for £120 and sold it around 12 months later for more than twice the cost, and in those days that was a fair old sum for me.

I did this by doing what my predecessor had failed to do. I told my customers who I was, what I was doing, when I was doing it and what was in it for them – consistently.

Whenever you do a job – go all out to show you are successful. Whatever you do, prove your interest, ability and faith by doing it well!

**Always make your potential customers aware of you.**

# Look at all the angles. Turn your business upside-down, back-to-front and inside-out

**I** once owned a hotel on the edge of an industrial estate in Walsall. Not what you would call a romantic setting. The hotel was more or less running at full capacity on week days, but nearly empty on weekends. It was considered by all to be a commercial hotel, period.

Not to me, I decided that we could become a wedding venue. Within 12 months we were hosting three weddings on weekends, becoming the busiest wedding hotel in the area whilst remaining a busy commercial hotel during the week.

Others were not prepared to see the hotel other than what it already was, a commercial hotel by an industrial estate. We had 100 bedrooms, we had banqueting suites, we had bars, we had car parks and we had good staff – that's a wedding hotel and a lot more, right!

I created 34 four-poster bridal suites for 'A honeymooners paradise' and introduced romantic dinner dances every Saturday. To provide a balance for the romantic and family trade we added a Health Hydro with swimming pool, whirlpool, steamrooms and saunas. It could well have been a top tourist spot. The increase in business was later rewarded, I sold the hotel for many millions.

Take a look at your business, what business are you really in? I recently read of a company in the north east that had for years been making nuts and bolts for the ship building industry. All their customers were ship builders, yet the company, if asked, would say they were in the nuts and bolts industry.

New management decided on a different view, they were in the ship building industry. This change of view led to the company progressing to record levels of profit by using their expertise in 'metal bashing' to manufacture other metal based products for their existing customer base.

For every action there's a reaction. Move a wall to make one room larger, then the next room becomes smaller!

So do an overall projection — plan ahead.

Not only for what you want now, but also for what you would eventually like in the future. Always ensure that appropriate windows or doors are in the right place at the first build stage, to make "easy access" links to connect the subsequent extension phases.

Always try to obtain the maximum possible planning permissions that you think you may require before you start building, especially with a listed property! Planners like you to save it, but in theory would prefer you to save it as it was.

## Don't ever miss obvious moves.

## For every action there's a reaction.

## Package your product to your customers' requirements.

# Future Opportunities & Staying In Business

Starting a business and getting it up and running is quite a different skill to staying in business and maintaining growth. As with everything else, the initial excitement and adventure and the extra energy they provide can eventually wear off.

When your business is up and running, its main enemies are not understanding the skills required and complacency. Margaret Thatcher said, "It's easy to start something, it's keeping it going that's difficult".

Some people, especially from sales backgrounds, have all the skills required to get a company off the ground but fail to become good enough managers to keep a company in business. Many of them fall down through:

1. Lack of organising ability.

2. Inability to plan ahead.

3. Lack of leadership and management ability.

4. Not maintaining a positive attitude to sustain future success.

5. Inadequate use of staff resources.

You will need all these skills, be honest with yourself, it's not an admission of defeat if you are lousy at implementing and maintaining systems or if you are disorganised – some of the best business people fall down in these areas.

The biggest mistake is to think you're good at what you're not. Of course you can and should work on your weaknesses, but this is when you should be team building, employing people who have the skills to improve the areas you fall short on.

Take a look at any top businessperson – it may be their style, charm, charisma and effort that has breathed life into a company and continues to front it. But take a look behind this front and you'll generally find top managers, experts in their particular field, holding down systems and operations.

When employing managers, look to employ someone who has the skills you need for future progression. This is easy to say, but sometimes difficult in practice. We all have a tendency to employ people we like, mostly because they are similar to ourselves. You don't need another you, you need someone who can help maintain the business you control. Someone who is good enough to make it even better.

**Back up the people who back you up.**

**If you cannot change your shortfalls – employ somebody who can.**

# Continued Future Success

**W**hen you are successful your ambitions will make you want even more success. By now you'll have a far greater knowledge of your business, what it entails and what you have to give it. In addition, you will have a reputation carefully nurtured for success.

If you've done a good job, you'll have a good team in place and the business will be generating extra business based on your reputation. This does not mean that life gets so easy that you don't have to work at it any more. Far from it, the emphasis of your efforts change but by now you'll have more funds, both business and personal.

Always remember that if a company is not moving forward it's going out of business, until you start taking it forward again.

**A business is like a pet, it dies if you stop feeding it!**

**Enjoy the fun but never stand still.**

# What do you do once you have made it? Make sure you always enjoy it!

**M**oney does not automatically buy happiness. It does, however, enable you to enjoy the trappings of success. Use it wisely to give happiness to others and yourself.

Do not ever let success make you greedy and jealous of others who are more successful. Be proud of your success but don't be a show-off.

Remember the bad times you had. Continue to save for a rainy day and do not overstretch yourself.

Do not let money be the total goal of your success. Concentrate on being successful and money will follow you. Continually strive to make your future successes even greater.

### Enjoy the contentment that success can give to you.

# A short story entitled
# What Made Me?

**Well, who would have imagined it? Young Stevie Joynes one day giving advice on how to be successful in life! But somehow I did it.**

**So I thought, 'what if I could pinpoint what made me what I am and gave me my main personality traits?'**

**So I sketched out a little scenario of my life – and here it is!**

My Mom and Dad obviously had something to do with it, but after that it seemed to be mainly due to outside influences. I remember my first seaside outing when I was 2½ years old. My dad and uncle each held my hand and took me for a paddle in the sea. I had my normal clothes on, less my shoes, and the waves kept lapping up my legs and trousers – they didn't seem to notice, but I did. Could I really depend totally on adults? I finished up shivering and blue, without trousers, and my sister's knickers on!

## Lesson learnt:
*Look out for yourself as early as you can.*


When I was five years old, I caught diphtheria. Mom and Dad sat on the edge of the bed and said that I was going to the country in an ambulance to get better. I thought, well, the neighbours, who usually watched everything from their doorsteps with their arms folded, would see me carried out on a stretcher – that would make a big impact, I would be a hero! But the nurse said: "Oh, you're only a little dot" and carried me out in her arms like a baby.

## Lesson learnt:
*Life doesn't always go to plan.*


In the isolation hospital, I was kept in bed. A big, spiteful nurse took a dislike to me, even in the tiny bedroom which I shared with one other older patient. She said: "Look at him, he listens to every word we say". I turned my head to the wall, with no other escape.

## Lesson learnt:
*Never be nasty, spiteful or cruel to people. **It hurts!***


Coming out of hospital about six weeks later, in a wheelchair on the bus (I had lost the use of my legs), I asked my sister if I could have some of those beautiful flowers please. She said: "They're **dandelions**!". But I persuaded her to get me some.

## Lesson learnt:
*The world was still as beautiful and I could still make an impact upon my own life.*

I caught scarlet fever! **Same isolation hospital! Same nasty nurse!** She made me drink sour milk and tormented me in many other ways.

## Lesson learnt:
*I survived last time – I could do it again.*

### The Biggest Downturn
That nurse made me keep a low profile, **to say nothing and try not to be noticed.** This became a habit and stopped me asking questions at school; therefore I did not learn the basics of maths that had been taught while I was away ill – they assumed I knew them and never taught me! Maths was the first lesson each morning – it was a disaster I dreaded. I used to hope that during assembly my mother would arrive and take me to the dentist. I also hated dentists, but not as much as maths. I had a reasonable day **if nobody noticed me**.

## Lesson learnt:
*Although it didn't occur to me until I was about thirteen – if you don't know, ask someone who does, and learn it.*

### Most of my school years until about age thirteen

I was pretty sickly and took lots of time off school. I liked making plasticine soldiers and cowboys, creating whole villages of people and animals. I liked reading, mainly about the Romans, and also about finding buried treasure in the ruins of the Aztecs and Incas – I had an exciting life.

### Lesson learnt:

*How to be creative and enjoy the excitement of a life that I would be in charge of one day in the future – making my own opportunities.*

### Aged thirteen to fifteen

I suddenly woke up; I was no longer sickly. I obtained a second-hand Charles Atlas course. This, together with an old back axle used as weights, suddenly changed me from being totally emaciated to a fit, strong youth with **muscles and confidence**. I was ready for anything – and with my background, I felt that nothing could really be **that bad** ever again. I would soon pursue the opportunities that would **change my lifestyle – and change my life**.

### Lesson learnt:

*All those wasted years – never again. Find yourself as soon as you can, then continue to improve and make the most of every opportunity and every moment.*

### Aged fifteen to eighteen

I left school and started a new life. My first career choice would have been as an archaeologist; unfortunately, **no education** and **no sponsor** – **no chance**. My first job was as a plasterer's improver with my father. After that, I kept moving: two cabinet-making jobs, railways as a cleaner, then a bar boy (making money), then general building, especially carpentry. I enjoyed my life and my lifestyle – dance halls, laughing, having fun, being appreciated at work and learning about life's opportunities.

### Lesson learnt:

*If at first you don't succeed, then try and try again. When one door closes another one opens. Create your own destiny and progress it.*

### Aged eighteen to twenty-one

An intelligence, not education, test! I passed for National Service in the Royal Air Force. Now I was in the fast lane, learning and making up for the education I had missed in the past. I did maths Crammer lessons, plus additional correspondence courses in Psychology and the National School of Salesmanship. I was leading a very full life.

### Lesson learnt:

*It's never too late to learn – use your new knowledge to progress yourself and change your future forever.*

### Aged twenty-one and onwards

Another new life – back to civvy street. Not quite the total change that I had expected. I returned to the job that I had left, but now I had the determination to make something of myself – back to the building trade but with high hopes of progress. I took days off, wore a suit and applied for sales positions. Continual interviews taught me what they were looking for – I adapted and played the part. I was **fast, willing, enthusiastic** and **nothing was ever too much trouble.** The Business Opportunities column in the local paper became my favourite read. Perhaps I could take a shorter cut to success – a mobile Fish & Chip van, £120 o.n.o. – within my price range. I bought it, redecorated it, marketed it as Steve's Chippery and started another fast learning curve, operating it on a shoestring. Unfortunately, nature intervened and put me in hospital for six weeks with agonisingly swollen knees and ankles. In the bed next to me was a young salesman and from him I obtained information regarding the actual requirements needed to **be a salesman**. I decided I could be even better than him; I sold my van for twice what I had paid and obtained my first sales job as an office equipment salesman.

## Lesson learnt:
*Make sure that everything, no matter how bad, happens for the best. That spell in hospital gave me the invaluable information needed for my sales career – my tutor was in the next bed.*

Because I remembered how difficult it was to get my first sales job, despite taking the National School of Salesmanship course, I wrote *Selling Yourself*, a simple guideline on how to obtain a position in sales and succeed in selling. I advertised this in the local paper, but it resulted in me selling only a few dozen copies. I then created *Friendships Unlimited*, a friendship and marriage bureau, fifteen shillings for 3 months membership. I discovered that the papers would not advertise this [possibly] dubious enterprise so I advertised it in 6p-a-week shop windows. It was ahead of its time (well before Dateline) and the applications were mainly from men. I sent my girlfriend's name and address as a stop-gap until I could attract more female applications – but they were generally too shy to apply.

## Lesson learnt:

*Think your idea through fully **before commencing it**. Make certain you have enough cash to market your **bright** ideas properly. **Don't give up too early**.*

### I wanted faster progress

I was moving from one sales job to another at a fast pace: selling credit drapery, trading stamps, advertising space, then Eskimo Frozen Foods (company van, some commission and clients who sometimes wanted to buy before I sold them something).

## Lesson learnt:
*If you missed out on a formal education, then teach yourself and learn in the fast track.* **Never forget the past but always improve on the future***.*

### Aged twenty-six

Another gigantic step – I bought another business, a café. Keeping my position as the Midlands Sales Supervisor for Eskimo Foods, my overheads were minimal, all of my takings would be surplus to my normal requirements. I totally refurbished the café into the "Golden Grill". Grills all day – a McDonald's before its time – it did quite well during the day but practically nothing in the evening. The owner of a small local hotel asked me if I would do evening meals for their bed and breakfast guests. I said yes but decided that a hotel (with people paying for a bed) sounded more profitable and glamorous than a café. So I sold it – for twice its cost – and bought a guest house.

## Lesson learnt:
*Make the most of any opportunity; adapting and changing your life for your future benefit.*

### A guest house I developed into the Midland Hotel

This was my first real venture into freehold property. I was on the 'property development ladder' and this was just right for me. I could rebuild and adapt most of it myself, keeping my overheads low by working as a salesman during the day in my smart suit – dirty jeans at night and weekends.

## Lesson learnt:
*Don't let the grass grow under your feet.*
*Do what you know you can be good at and keep your*
*overheads as low as possible.*

### Yet another hotel

The Midland Hotel, at the back of the railway station in Walsall, was an Oasis in the Wilderness and extremely successful – its 13 bedrooms were let to regulars many weeks ahead. I decided to create another hotel, but on a larger scale. I bought a private school on the main Birmingham Road, borrowing most of the money from the sellers, to be paid in full from the sale of the Midland. I thank the Lord quite often, but this is one time that I remember asking him to help me. Whilst walking through the park, I said: "Please Lord, find someone to buy the Midland Hotel so that I can pay for the County and have enough finance to develop it". It happened – thank you.

I was carried away by my own enthusiasm and nearly overstretched myself. My back-up plan was to do the County on a smaller scale. I continued selling Autobar vending machines, my 'commission only' earnings paying the bricklayers, etc. I was Salesman of the Year in 1965.

I became a full-time hotelier when I opened the County Hotel. It was a tremendous success and I constantly expanded it. More bedrooms, bigger bars, conference rooms and a bigger restaurant. I was then approached by another builder and we merged our interests at our own personal valuations, forming Develop & Prosper Holdings Ltd, buying and developing the Chateau Impney Hotel in Droitwich. We sold our assets 2½ years later. My share turned out to be less than the increased property value of the County Hotel.

## Lesson learnt:
*Sometimes you can take short-cuts and try to run too fast. A partnership is like a marriage – you need a very special partner*

### My next venture – the Barons Court Hotel
I was independent again, with more capital than ever before, so it was on to the next chapter. I was once again in full personal control of my own destiny.

On the site of a run-down nightclub I created another oasis in a wilderness – **100 bedrooms, restaurants, bars, health hydro** and a **nightclub**. A possible road widening scheme had resulted in no developments along this main road; mine was the first. Fourteen years and fourteen extensions later, the planners did me a favour. They said: "No more planning unless you buy some more land, with roads on two sides, a canal at the back and a quarry at the other side". This was impossible. I started looking for another site. One of the many agents I contacted said he also had a **stately home** for sale. A **Stately Home**! Could you really buy a **Stately Home**? Well, I did, and created the only Spa Resort in a stately home, an ongoing story that keeps growing on me.

### Lesson learnt:
*Listen and learn, be prepared to accept the inevitable and steer an alternative course. Because I was too busy to run it, I sold Barons Court for over £8 million, six months after buying **Hoar Cross Hall**. Thank you Lord! It was perfect timing, just before a deep recession.*

# Key Pointers to Success

* Always be Dependable, Happy and Hardworking

* Treat others the way you would like to be treated yourself

* Be an interested listener

* Always have Plenty of Optimism and Enthusiasm

* Have a Zest for Life and a Willing Smile

* Take actions to make everything for the best, giving your business whatever it needs!

* Keep looking for opportunities

* Don't let small disappointments spoil the good parts

* Enjoy the excitement

* Make your business your favourite hobby

* Upgrade your life – but never forget your roots

* Always remember – health and happiness is in the mind

* Heaven is a healthy, happy, contented mind

* It will continue naturally when you get there

ॐ

I now continue with my favourite hobby; creating beautiful buildings that are appreciated **by my guests**. I couldn't become an archaeologist and discover **ancient Rome** but, instead, I build my own versions of the **pleasure baths** and **spas** of **ancient Rome** and **Greece**.

With our Resort and Day Spa, and another Day spa, who knows what I will do next? Meanwhile, I am enjoying every moment of the happiness I can provide for others.

Take Action

# Section Three – Keeping Going

# Action these basic principles if at any time you feel you're slipping and need to pull your socks up

You would not expect a sailor to reach his destination by leaving port and letting his ship drift, he has to navigate and pre-plan his voyage – so do you

* **Determination is your vehicle to success.**

* **Belief is the fuel for your determination.**

* **Success comes from believing and taking action.**

* **Thought – everything you do is ruled by the way you think, it governs the way you act. Think continually about what improvements you can make. The more you think about being successful then the more successful you will be. The more you think about failing then the quicker it will happen. You become what you think about.**

* **Adventure is an inconvenience rightly considered.**

* **Inconvenience is an adventure wrongly considered.**

* **Don't stop doing things because you're getting older. You will get older if you stop doing things.**

* All your problems have a cause. Act to remove the root cause and the problem will disappear.

* Justify the faith others have in you.

* Success is a journey – not a destination.

* Be proud of your ambitions and success.

Be – Optimistic – Confident – Cheerful – Always.

Remember the real challenge in life is not just getting what you want! It's also continuing to want what you already have!

# Basic principles you should always follow

* Carefully pre-plan your success – it will only happen if you do.

* Have confidence in your business – it is a direct reflection of you and your good ideas.

* In management always be firm, friendly but not familiar.

* Treat everyone the way you would like to be treated yourself.

* Maintain your integrity.

* Always provide value for money.

* Do not cheat people. Your reputation is too important.

* Be proud of your personal values or change them until you can be proud.

* Do not take everyone at face value, there may be a hidden agenda – 'they would say that wouldn't they'.

* Always keep an open mind – the opportunities out there will surprise you.

* Any major expansion puts a strain on cash flow.

# Eleven First Steps

1. Read this book – it will not make you successful by itself, but it will help.

2. Decide what you want, then write down an action plan on how you are going to achieve it – do you really want your dreams to come true?

3. Decide when you want to start taking action.

4. Make a definite decision to change the habits that are stopping you getting there. Do what you have to do to make your dreams come true.

5. Go for it. Start making small changes straight away. It will be like getting on to a conveyor belt – you start slowly, making decisions for all the steps you have to take. Then taking them!

6. Read the book again, keep making notes of actions and changes required to ensure your progress.

7. Continually improve and retrain yourself. Move further and faster along the conveyor. Always remembering to keep looking and thinking about the stage you're at and check you're moving in the right direction. Be prepared to change and fine tune your plan

8.  Keep a close check on your funding requirements.

9.  Keep your financial outlays to a minimum.

10. Make things happen for you instead of letting things happen to you.

11. Keep smiling – keep your sense of humour, laugh at yourself sometimes and enjoy every moment of your life.

**Change your lifestyle - change your life.**

# Knowing what's right for you

I have progressed in life to an unbelievable extent compared to my initial hopes and dreams. Occasionally, my health has suffered through my endeavours but I can confirm the problems I endured and conquered were always well worth the effort and the final benefits are a most welcome conclusion.

If, after reading this book, you really feel that a large number of the basic qualifications necessary for success are out of your reach, then you may be happier making a success in other areas of your life.

Count yourself lucky, you've found out now without the inconvenience and heartache.

I wish you every success, whatever it means to you, the least we all deserve is to "be happy".

**Enjoy the rest of your life.**

# Health through happiness

**W**elcome to a life with a happy healthy mind and body. Follow the Joynes Family "Happiness Philosophy" – a simple method for mental peace. Smile and wish people well, not because you are familiar, but because you are happy and friendly and wish them to feel the same, you will then spread this happiness, continuing the subconscious contented well-being attitude, for that "Feel-Good" factor we all desire.

Nature endows us with our initial face and figure potential! From around the age of five, we start to create our own finished version – **a reflection of our own personality, character and attitude to life always shines through!**

Happiness and eventual contentment is the greatest medicine of all – they allow the mind and body to improve and heal themselves, the more we use this friendly attitude the more we will enrich our own lives and the lives of others.

Think well of yourself and try to do the same with others take and make time to care for each other.

Always enjoy life as you progress through it. If you miss your train, then accept it and take advantage of the spare time you have. Enjoy a nice cup of coffee or browse in a book shop instead of increasing your blood pressure by fuming away.

Life is certainly the best free gift we're ever going to be given. Make the most of it, do not waste it and do not abuse it.

Think yourself younger and smile about it – people will soon notice a difference.

**"Be kind and gentle to those around you"**

**"Don't just want what you want, also continue to want what you already have"**

**"Be fair and honest with yourself and you will eventually become what you think you are"**

**"Count your blessings – not your problems"**

**"Most of all, be happy and keep smiling"**

# Balance your mind and body

The body reacts to pressure and stress and tells us to slow down by taking action against our weakest parts. You will also need to take action to rectify the situation with simple relaxation techniques allowing the body and mind to rebalance. Repay your mind and body for the hard work they put in and they will repay you with many more hours; of happiness and the ability to work harder without unnecessary illness and fatigue.

**Take care of your health**
**as well as your wealth.**

# Take every opportunity to market your products and services

Bearing in mind my advice to always fully use a marketing opportunity...

As you progress, make spaces to treat yourself to regular time-out relaxation. Regenerate your mind and body whenever you need it, in the wonderful setting of:

HOAR CROSS HALL

THE ONLY SPA RESORT IN A STATELY HOME

*Enjoy the Fresh Air*

Enjoy that special luxury "Time to yourself" – unwind and relax, finding warm hospitality in the heart of the countryside – fresh air, beautiful flowers and bird songs.

Switch off and recuperate in the opulent surroundings of this grand Stately Home with its gilded ceilings and fine furnishings, set quietly amongst parkland with fountains and formal gardens.

A world of fun and relaxation, where caring professionals offer advice to each individual, allowing you to build up your own personal programme of supervised activity, interspersed with periods of relaxation or exercise and your own choice of additional treatments.

Palatial interiors convey an atmosphere of comfort and happiness, find space and friendly relaxation. From the sumptuously restored long gallery and drawing room, card room and converted chapel to the champagne bar (originally the library) discreetly hidden for those who wish to avoid it. The oak panelled Jacobean staircase leads to more than 90 individually appointed en-suite bedrooms, suites, penthouse suites and the fantastic Royal Suite.

A Spa creation that never quite stands still. "That would be unfair to you" – and your future relaxation and happiness.

Enjoy your stay at your Stately Home escape, a rare combination of elegance and pleasure, offering personal contentment at your own pace.

*Long Gallery*

***Hydrotherapy Swimming Pool***

Enjoy total relaxation – you deserve it!

Find an unusual combination of hot and cold water relaxation opportunities. Treat your mind and body to time-out with pampering treatments and complete enjoyment.

*Cocktail Bar (originally the library). Discreetly hidden should you wish to avoid it, over 3,000 old books to browse through at your leisure.*

*Golf Academy*

*Life's still all go!*

# THE ONLY SPA RESORT
# IN A STATELY HOME
# KEEPS GROWING

## "THE BEGINNING"

**1989:** Hoar Cross Hall purchased as a semi, derelict Stately Home then we doubled its size adding pool, spa treatment rooms, aerobics, gymnasium, bedrooms and suites, reclaiming formal gardens, new tennis courts, croquet and boules.

**1991:** Opened as the Premier Stately Home Health Spa.

**1992:** Final Completion of the west wing extension.

**1993:** Extension trebling size of the gymnastic and aerobics areas.

**1994:** West wing relaxation area and further therapy `suites.

**1995:** Golf Academy opened with PGA professional, garden room, an elegant rest area (now the quiet room).

**1996:** New spa reception and additional treatment rooms. Plantation Restaurant extension.

**1997:** Further additional treatment rooms created to meet demand. Larger changing rooms.

**1998:** Beauty makeover area.

**1999:** New aerobic studio, larger gymnasium

Additional bedrooms, suites & Royal Suite, complimentary water grotto massage treatment, yoga suite, alternative therapy floor with Ayur Veda, new boutique and product shop, oasis and garden room with terrace

Take Action

**2000:** Balance of grounds reclaimed and landscaped.

## 2003/4: The creation of relaxation

The new amenities at Hoar Cross Hall should open in late 2004, over 65,000 sq ft of luxurious pampering.

Steve Junior came up with another idea: "let's build another Eden at Hoar Cross Hall" – he now had a proven model of success and wanted to repeat it. Why not take advantage of the space and beautiful setting of our Stately Home Spa Resort? Adding to it and creating all the amenities available at Eden Day Spa. We obtained planning for a wonderful extension.

The size was equivalent to the total of all of the previous eight extensions carried out over a ten-year period. We were no longer simply adding facilities to meet our guests' requests, we were going to remove any crush and give them everything they had ever asked for. Including: upgrading the Golf Academy and adding a 9-hole golf course to the driving range, plus the new soft ball game area and squash courts.

Another exciting chapter in our family lives.

The Eden Management team were eager to oversee the operation of the new Eden at Hoar Cross Hall and the Resort Management were just as excited to be able to operate the upgraded Spa Resort. More luxurious bedrooms and suites, including the Princess Suite for four, Hot Tub and Sauna, more space everywhere for our happy guests to relax in, with separate welcome and check-in areas for Resort Residents and Day guests. The opportunity to use every added amenity plus an even greater range of relaxation pursuits in the new Yoga Suite and additional Aerobics Suite, an extended Gymnasium complemented by the 25-metre salt water swimming pool and whirlpools, Tepidarium, Sauna Steam Room, Saunarium, Aqua Detox Temple and additional Water Grotto, additional hot and cold pulse jet showers, walk-in douche plunge, hot and cold walks, Spa pools and massage jets, heated relaxation couches on the bridge over the pool with a swim-in cave (music and star-lights below).

Time to meditate and enjoy the switch-off or get up and get motivated by welcoming instructors. Separate restaurants for Resort Residents and Day guests means more space for relaxed dining, even a licensed Continental Café to complete the day – a total escape.

Complemented by an Italian Roof Garden, adding a

new facet of outdoor relaxation on the opposite side to the Formal Gardens and with easy access to the Garden Room, Boutique and Product Shop goodies "especially for you and your friends, old and new".

The original Grotto with Saunarium, massage jets and Aromatherapy room adjoins the Hydro pool and Spa and many relaxation retreats. The Continental Café serves drinks and treats throughout the day, as does the Garden Room.

**Resort Residents and Day Guests will have separate Reception Check-in and Check-out areas, separate Changing Rooms and separate Restaurants. All guests will enjoy more space, colonnaded Atrium, Lounges, etc.**

The New Me boutique has an exciting array of quality clothes to suit all ages including fun toys for children.

# "THE FUTURE"

We have now created all of the Relaxation and Fun amenities that our guests have requested, fulfilling all of your known requirements for the foreseeable future.

We don't know for certain what steps we will take next; if we did we would probably have done it already. We do however continue to listen and learn about our guest's wishes. Our aim for the foreseeable future is to continue giving our guests satisfaction. "We are extremely happy that our guests keep returning to relax and enjoy life at this "Beautiful Stately Home Spa Resort".

My next personal goal is to work hard at aiming to be a hundred, with far too many intentions and projects to allow anything to interrupt it, giving happiness and contentment to all around me and having too many current achievement wishes to ever be bored with this wonderful life.

# *A day is all it takes......*
## *at*

THE CREATION OF RELAXATION
### NEWARK, NOTTINGHAMSHIRE

*The Family at Eden Hall a few months before it was completed for take off*

The first most luxurious Day Spa in the UK, a unique environment designed exclusively for ladies and gentlemen wishing to experience a full day of relaxation for the mind, exercise for the body and total pampering for the soul . . .

Enjoy another "different world" – the creation of relaxation and happiness beyond your imagination. A world that satisfies all of your senses, colours which calm, an atmosphere that relaxes, sounds which soothe, aromas that stimulate and tastes that delight.

*Detoxify in the Aqua Temple*

*Eden Hall* has been beautifully extended and restored to a cool Mediterranean design. Amidst gushing waterfalls, fountains, statues and flora you will find an oasis of tranquillity, also housing one of the largest saltwater vitality swimming pool in the UK. This superb facility provides an array of therapies to massage and stimulate every muscle. Breathe in the fresh air of the countryside no matter what the weather in the connecting outdoor relaxation pool. The adjacent Aqua Temple is most beneficial to your circulation, detoxifying to the body, cleansing for the skin and a fun area for your overall well-being with saunas, steam rooms, herbal temple, saunarium, crushed ice, tropical and mist showers all complemented by additional therapeutic water experiences for your further relaxation.

*Time to relax and reflect.....*

*Eden*'s blissful treatments have been designed simply to help you achieve "the way you want to feel", these are administered by caring therapists mainly using the Elemis product range.

Relaxation, visualisation and meditation classes allow you to escape into your very own dream world. In contrast the fully equipped gymnasium, on two floors dividing the resistance machines from cardio-vascular equipment, and the aerobic exercise class studio provide the ideal physical antidote to stress.

*..... or simply relax*

Dining is a delight in the Seventh Heaven restaurant comprised of four beautifully decorated rooms featuring stunning ceilings, two of which are 25 feet high, original fireplaces, marble designs and stained glass windows. Its tantalising grand buffet style menu serves a deliciously healthy choice.

Various relaxing lounges allow you to find peace and freedom away from any hustle and bustle including two vast "palm house" conservatories, all waiting to comfort you.

*Mellow out*

Simply choose a full day's experience according to "The Way You Want To Feel".

*Salt water vitality*

Take Action

*A warm friendly welcome awaits*

# Buy your favourite person

# HOAR CROSS HALL

*The only Spa Resort in a Stately Home*

Hoar Cross, Near Yoxall, Staffordshire DE13 8QS

For Reservations, Gift Vouchers and Enquiries
Tel: 01283 575671 Fax: 01283 575652

www.hoarcross.co.uk Email: info@hoarcross.co.uk

# Enjoy the splendour of